VETS ON ANIMAL REIKI

THE POWER OF
Animal Reiki Healing in Veterinary Practice

Presented by
THE SHELTER ANIMAL REIKI ASSOCIATION

Foreword by
KATHLEEN PRASAD

Copyright © 2019 Shelter Animal Reiki Association.

All rights reserved. No part of this publication may be reproduced, stored in a retrieval system, or transmitted in any form or by any means without the prior written permission of Ms. Prasad, nor be otherwise circulated in any form of binding or cover other than that in which it is published.

Published in the United States by: Shelter Animal Reiki Association
ISBN-978-1-095295-3-4

Book Design & Production: VMC Art & Design, LLC

DISCLAIMER: The suggestions in this manual are not intended as a substitute for professional veterinary care. Reiki sessions are given for the purpose of stress reduction and relaxation to promote healing. Reiki is not a substitute for medical diagnosis and treatment. Reiki practitioners do not diagnose conditions nor do they prescribe, perform medical treatment, nor interfere with the treatment of a licensed medical professional. It is recommended that animals be taken to a licensed veterinarian or licensed health care professional for any ailment they have.

Table of Contents

Foreword i

An Introduction to Animal Reiki 6

Christina Chambreau, DVM, CVH 13

Patricia Jordan, DVM 33

Marc Malek, DVM 57

Ricardo Garé, DVM 79

The Tree of Life for Animals (TOLFA) 97

Animal Reiki Practitioner Code of Ethics 102

The Shelter Animal Reiki Association 106

"Remus Teachings"

The sun rose, as it does every morning,
the mist kissing its essence upon the fields,
and my journey took a new dawning.

I sighed.

My soul lifted by the long awaited call
of the animals I had yet to meet
and in love with which I'd fall.

Enriched by the women from the far flung corners
of our globe
that would forever join us,

By the teachings my soul hears and already knows,
its magic source,
its ebbs and flows.

I connected to that source

that wave of light, of love
of compassion, of force

that grasps my very soul,
enlightens my true self
and takes its hold.

I'll forever stand barefoot in these fields
as the energy continues to yield

for me inside my soul and heart,
a mystery, a story,
but mostly, a place from which to start.

Blessed am I to say these things aloud,
my mirrored teachers bow their heads—
I can only do my best to make them proud.

—Rebecca Westwood

The above poem is a contemplation on Animal Reiki inspired by the animals of Remus Memorial Horse Sanctuary in England.

Rebecca Westwood qualified as a Registered Veterinary Nurse (RVN) in 2005 and has volunteered for charities around the world promoting animal welfare, nursing, and practice management as well as working in various United Kingdom veterinary practices training student veterinary nurses. She is passionate about practicing veterinary medicine with a holistic approach and owns a home visit vet practice doing that work with her vet husband. In addition, she has a healing practice called Peace. Heal. Love. Rebecca has trained with Kathleen Prasad and like Kathleen, strongly believes that animals should be given the right to choose their own healing. She has seen firsthand the power of Reiki in hospitalized patients who are recovering post-surgery and with other animals with all kinds of emotional and physical ailments.

Foreword

WHAT EXACTLY IS REIKI? HOW DOES IT SUPPORT healing? These are not easy questions to answer, but science has begun to shed light on the subtle yet profound effects of this expanding holistic modality. The National Institutes of Health (NIH) has funded a number of peer-reviewed studies on Reiki for humans and animals over the past twenty years, and the results are promising[1]. From these studies, we now know that Reiki activates the parasympathetic nervous system and can reduce stress and lessen pain, anxiety, and depression in humans and reduce stress in animals. These studies have also shown that Reiki can increase self-esteem and the general quality of life. The results of these peer-reviewed studies have been supplemented by thousands of anecdotal success stories. Today, Reiki is being successfully used as a complementary (not alternative) support for humans in hospitals, nursing homes, and hospice centers, and for animals in veterinary clinics, animal shelters, and animal sanctuaries all over the world. Based on the promising scientific findings along with the inspiring

---

1. See a review of 13 peer-reviewed scientific studies of Reiki from 1998-2016: https://www.ncbi.nlm.nih.gov/pmc/articles/PMC5871310/.

anecdotal cases, the best care for our animals would include the perfect combination of conventional medicine and Animal Reiki.

This book features interviews with four medically trained veterinarians who have practiced Animal Reiki for decades with great success—who better to bridge the gap between scientific understanding and anecdotal evidence than highly trained and experienced veterinarians. The personal and powerful testimonials of these veterinarians should encourage all of us, veterinarians and lay practitioners alike, to investigate the positive benefits of adding Animal Reiki to any animal's treatment protocol. As the variety of perspectives in this book demonstrates, Animal Reiki can be a beautiful addition to any veterinarian's toolbox.

ANIMAL REIKI FOR THE VETERINARIAN

It's important to make a distinction, especially in the context of this book, in the way a veterinarian practices Animal Reiki and the way a lay practitioner would and should practice. Veterinarians make their treatment decisions based on their extensive medical training in the diagnosis and treatment of specific disease processes, as well as on their specialty medical training, degrees, and additional licensing courses. All of this education affects the way veterinarians approach the healing process. However, as you will read in this book, veterinarians trained in Animal Reiki are able to combine their use of Reiki with their medical training, and this combination brings with it beautiful and amazing healing possibilities!

ANIMAL REIKI FOR NON-VETERINARIANS

For the Animal Reiki lay practitioner, it is most important to abide by the Animal Reiki Practitioner Code of Ethics, which I authored in 2008. This Code sets apart our profession as a meditative, non-medical practice that does not diagnose and does not interfere with the practice of veterinary medicine in any way. Practitioners are not required to take medical/anatomical training because the meditative approach is always the same, no matter what health issue an animal faces. The Code of Ethics encourages Animal Reiki practitioners to simply support the healing program prescribed by veterinarians with the addition of Animal Reiki when asked. It reminds all parties involved that Animal Reiki does not take the place of medical treatment. The Code is also very important in that it takes an even bigger step forward in human/animal relations by honoring animals as healers and teachers in their own right. These are qualities often overlooked by most humans. Practicing Animal Reiki helps all practitioners to awaken to the wisdom and gifts animals bring to the healing process through the many lessons in life—presence, forgiveness, courage, and more—that they teach us.

WHAT IS THE SHELTER ANIMAL REIKI ASSOCIATION (SARA)?

The Shelter Animal Reiki Association (SARA) is a non-profit organization that teaches and promotes meditation practices to create a peaceful, healing environment within shelters and other animal care settings. Our worldwide members work closely with staff and volunteers of animal organizations and veterinary practices to create a positive healing space for all.

Over the ten years SARA has been in existence, we have created powerful relationships with Animal Reiki practitioners and teachers as well as animal care professionals in many parts of world through our classes, publications, and other outreach. Our gentle, respectful Animal Reiki approach has been accepted by dozens of animal shelters, sanctuaries, and rescue centers—even those that support the most traumatized animals. We have seen firsthand how Animal Reiki can relieve stress and bring about a more peaceful state in rescued animals of varying species, health issues, and backgrounds. With these healing successes in mind, SARA has nurtured relationships and alliances with like-minded animal lovers and professionals who are willing to expand the healing paradigm to include holistic modalities.

We are committed to upholding and promoting the healing power of compassionate presence through the Animal Reiki Practitioner Code of Ethics. We pride ourselves on the advancement of the welfare of animals and the professionalism of our vocation. We also follow the Let Animals Lead™ method, in order to assure competence, quality, and ethical standards in our profession.

The 6 Pillars of Practice for the Let Animals Lead™ approach are:

1. The practices are based on traditional Japanese Reiki techniques and philosophy.

2. Touch is used only when animals seek it out, and then only as a compassionate support.

3. Mental focus techniques develop an "All is Well" state of mind for the practitioner who sees the animal's perfection in the present moment, rather than focusing on what's "wrong."

4. Meditation is taught as a state of mind with flexible physical forms.

5. Animal Reiki is mindfulness meditation practiced "with" our animals, rather than an energy therapy done "to" them.

6. This method acknowledges and honors each animal as a spiritual teacher and healer in his/her own right. Practitioners learn to listen and become receptive to their spiritual wisdom and healing gifts.

Although all of our members are trained in the Let Animals Lead™ method, SARA welcomes all Reiki lineages into our association, and supports all backgrounds and practices of Reiki for humans. Our unique method and approach for animals is driven by an aspiration to support, protect, and honor the sensitivities and wisdom of animals, the expertise and knowledge of the veterinarians who care for them, and the tireless, brave work of animal rescue professionals.

We at SARA hope that this book can inspire new conversations and relationships between veterinarians and animal lovers and support the infinite healing potential of animals everywhere!

May the animals light your way,

Kathleen Prasad
President and Co-Founder,
The Shelter Animal Reiki Association (SARA)

An Introduction to Animal Reiki

WHAT IS REIKI?

Reiki is a Japanese meditation system created by Mikao Usui in the early 20th century. Reiki meditation helps us let go of anger, worry, fear, and stress to uncover our best self—one that is peaceful, grateful, compassionate, and in harmony with others. A Reiki practice helps us choose positivity and increases our ability to support others with compassion, even in difficult situations. Because animals communicate energetically, they love when we get peaceful through Reiki meditation, even when they are simply in the same room with us. However, because they are naturally in tune with the flow of energy, they are also affected by our emotions and mental state when we are not peaceful. In this way, our stress is contagious. If we are stressed, angry, or anxious, animals will sense this and be affected negatively by it. Yet if we are peaceful, this will affect the animals (and the people) around us in a positive way.

BENEFITS OF ANIMAL REIKI

Reiki is most often used as a supportive or complementary technique for human healing. As more people experience the benefits of Reiki for themselves, they want to share these benefits with their animal friends. As a result, the use of Reiki with animals is growing. Although the treatment approach with Animal Reiki is very different from how we offer Reiki to humans, the holistic benefits are the same: stress-relief and relaxation that promote self-healing on the physical, mental, emotional, and spiritual levels.

Learning Animal Reiki, with its meditative practices, is also beneficial for the practitioner. Meditation has been proven to be very healing for the body, mind, and spirit. Meditating with animals is even better! Animals are very intuitive. For that reason, they are more connected to nature and experience the interconnectedness of all beings. They are also gifted with the ability to live in the present moment, without all of the mental and emotional clutter than we humans struggle with, a struggle that often keeps us from feeling the oneness of all things. Meditating with animals through Reiki can more easily help us reconnect to the earth and to each present moment by helping us access a deeper sense of compassion.

WHAT DOES AN ANIMAL REIKI PRACTITIONER DO?

When animals are well, they naturally live in a space of balance and presence in each moment. It is this quality of pure presence and acceptance that our animals show us that provides us with so much support when we are ill. When they are suffering, either from emotional or physical trauma, just like us, they need support to get back to that place of balance and peace. Animal Reiki practitioners practice meditation to bring their energy into a balanced space. Reiki meditation helps us let go of anger and worry and instead radiate humility, honesty, and compassion. The inner qualities Reiki meditation creates within us feels comforting to the animals who are with us. While we meditate, animals are able to connect to us and enter a state of deep relaxation, which is the ideal condition for self-healing. Healing is not about curing but about supporting animals to access peace and wholeness in each moment, whatever issues they may be facing. Being present for another being with peace and compassion is the ultimate healing we can offer to each other. Animals intuitively understand this when they are with us, but we humans need the support of Reiki meditation to help us return this gift to our animals.

WHAT DOES A REIKI PRACTITIONER NOT DO?

Reiki sessions are given for the purpose of stress reduction and relaxation to promote healing. Reiki is not a substitute for medical diagnosis and treatment. Reiki practitioners do not diagnose conditions nor do they prescribe, perform medical treatment, or interfere with the treatment of a licensed medical professional. Reiki practitioners do not manipulate energy or control animals in any way: animals lead the process, connecting in the healing space only if and how they wish.

HOW CAN REIKI HELP ANIMALS?

Reiki is ideal for animals because it is gentle, non-invasive, painless, and stress-free. Its main purpose is to facilitate stress reduction, energy balance, and relaxation to promote healing. Just like humans, when an animal is peaceful (having a relaxed body, mind, and spirit) they are able to access their body/mind/spirit's ability to self-heal.

The system of Reiki is not a substitute for medical diagnosis or treatment. It is not about "curing" any physical issue. Sharing Reiki with others is a powerful way to walk through difficulty, illness, and suffering. Compassionate presence is always the best healer, no matter the situation. Animal Reiki gives us the tools to walk with strength through the animal's healing journey, no matter what the outcome is. Peace is possible in every moment, even those that are most difficult.

Because Reiki is a form of meditation, it is important to note that there are many studies that point out the healing benefits of meditation. Through meditation, we find a deep sense of peace and well-being that will:

- Help maintain health and well-being on the physical, mental, and emotional levels

- Help induce deep relaxation and stress relief

- Help accelerate healing

- Help reduce pain and inflammation

- Help reduce behavior problems and aggression

- Help us heal from past mental or physical trauma

- Help lessen the side effects of other medical treatments

- Help support the dying process

WHY REIKI IS AN IDEAL HOLISTIC THERAPY FOR ANIMALS

- It is gentle, noninvasive, painless, and stress-free.

- It addresses the issues that need it most, even when unknown to the practitioner.

- It can be shared hands-on or from a distance and adapted to any environment or any problem an animal may face.

- It can do no harm to either recipient or practitioner.

- Animals can control their participation in the treatment, thus becoming the decision-makers in their own process of healing.

WHAT CREATES A SUCCESSFUL ANIMAL REIKI TREATMENT?

A successful Animal Reiki treatment requires just two things: the focus of the practitioner on the meditation practice, and the animal's acceptance of sharing that space with the practitioner.

WHAT DOES A TYPICAL ANIMAL REIKI TREATMENT LOOK LIKE?

Every treatment is different as every animal will choose to share Reiki in his or her own way. However there are two main signs that an animal is accepting the treatment:

- Signs of relaxation (yawning, deep and relaxed breathing, sleeping, etc.)

- An ebb and flow of movement: the animal may move away from the practitioner then come back, lie down to rest then get up, and so on. This pattern may be repeated many times within the course of one 30-minute session.

Rarely, an animal may choose to reject a Reiki session. In these cases, the animal may display behaviors such as annoyance, aggravation, and/or nervousness, along with an inability to settle.

IS ANIMAL REIKI A "HANDS-ON" HEALING SYSTEM?

Although a human Reiki treatment usually consists of a series of hand positions lightly placed upon different parts of the body, an Animal Reiki treatment is approached very differently. When doing Reiki on an animal, it is best to treat from several feet away and allow the animal to come forward to receive hands-on treatment only if he or she is open to it. Many animals will actually place certain body parts into the hands of the practitioner to show where they need healing the most. Other animals will simply lie down several feet away and fall into a deep "Reiki nap."

Because Animal Reiki treatments are not dependent upon physical contact for success, they are ideal for use with shelter animals. Animals who are fearful, skittish, abused, or aggressive are ideal candidates for Reiki from a distance. Thus, practitioners can share Reiki quite successfully whether physical contact is used or not.

WHERE IS THE BEST LOCATION FOR AN ANIMAL TO RECEIVE A REIKI TREATMENT IN A SHELTER?

Reiki meditation can be shared from outside the animal's kennel or within a quiet room (one-on one with the animal). Reiki can also be given outdoors. Reiki can be offered to individual animals or to a group of animals. Specific conditions in each shelter will dictate the way Reiki is best offered to the animals there.

I have become a profound proponent

of every single person in the

world learning Reiki.

Christina Chambreau, DVM, CVH

SPARKS, MARYLAND

Dr. Christina Chambreau is a holistic veterinarian based in Sparks, Maryland who has been helping people with alternative holistic healing for over 37 years. Dr. Chambreau has extensive clinical experience using the healing practice of homeopathy with the animals that she treats. She has also been trained in Reiki and has had wonderful results using Reiki with her animal clients. We spoke with Dr. Chambreau about her experiences with Animal Reiki and her own journey with holistic medicine.

SARA: Thank you for speaking with us today, Dr. Chambreau. We know that your holistic animal practice has successfully treated many, many animals with homeopathy and Reiki, and we're really eager to hear more about that and about how you came to this kind of veterinary practice.

Dr. Chambreau: With pleasure. It's really quite a story. I graduated from veterinary school in 1980. I was 30 years old and didn't even know what a vegetarian was—shows how unholistic I was! However, I had done a two-day animal acupuncture class with the original U.S. founders of IVAS (International Veterinary Acupuncture Society), Dr. Grady Young and Dr. Marvin Cain, and then did a little research with it that didn't work and that was it. It was just sort of out the window.

Two years later, a year maybe after I graduated from veterinarian school, I was working at a small satellite clinic, and a client came in and asked me to draw blood and send the results to her homeopathic veterinarian. I said, "Sure," and did it—drew the blood—and then said, "Hey, what is homeopathy?" She introduced me to it, and I called the veterinarian, who had taken the very first class offered by British homeopathic veterinarian George McCloud for the National Center for Homeopathy for Veterinarians. Her vet sent me two homeopathic remedies and said that these were good for cats with bladder problems. At the time, I didn't know any better and so I didn't understand that he had not been trained well enough by Dr. McCloud to know that's not how we prescribe in homeopathy. Homeopathy is based on the principle that "like cures like" and the diagnosis matches the entire animal, so it's not based on treating a condition.

I set these funny-looking bottles with white pills in them on the shelf, and a few months later, my boss was seeing a cat that had been on antibiotics continuously for three years for a bladder problem. Any time they tried to stop, it didn't work, and they were now starting to look at euthanasia maybe down the line because of no response. I said, "Hey boss, I've got this stuff that the homeopathic doctor sent. You want to try it?"

He said, "Sure. You ask her [the pet's owner]." Well, I was fairly timid, and I went in and I said, "Hi. I heard that your cat is just not responding to these antibiotics. There's this homeopathic medicine that can help." She said, "Well, I'll try anything. Tell me more about it." "Well, I don't know anything more about it," but I did explain that a veterinarian in another city had sent it to me and the upshot was that one week of giving the homeopathic medicine probably twice a day—because I was very conventional back then—and the cat was off the antibiotics completely for the next nine months that I was at the practice.

This amazing success inspired me to start learning homeopathy. By 1987, I was doing one hundred percent homeopathy in my practice and had a telephone consulting practice. I started speaking—to 150 people for a PETA (People for the Ethical Treatment of Animals) hearing about homeopathy and 150 up in New Hampshire for the New Hampshire Dog Group. I was just speaking everywhere I could about homeopathy and beginning to learn about holistic medicine in general.

By then, I was being treated with homeopathy, and a few years after that, about 1990, I was given a homeopathic remedy that had been very carefully thought out, and within 24 hours I could not lift my right arm. I couldn't shift gears in my manual transmission. I had to teach my five-year-old daughter how to switch the gears while I did the clutch. I was in a lot of pain, couldn't write, couldn't pick up a pencil. Somebody said, "You know, you could go to the local health center and there's a gal there who does Reiki."

Now I went, "I'll try anything." I couldn't figure out why I gotten this shoulder problem. It didn't fit any of my symptoms; it didn't fit the homeopathic remedy I had been on. It didn't make sense. So I went in, and she did an hour-long Reiki session, and I was sixty percent better. I could shift gears, I could write with my pen. I was very impressed with Reiki.

Then I went on to do other things, working with that shoulder, et cetera, but more importantly to share here, she called me the next day and said, "I usually don't call people, but I always do a Distant Reiki follow-up for every patient and your liver grabbed onto me for 20 minutes, so I thought I'd better call you." All of a sudden it made sense. A lot of my general issues stemmed from a past accident where I had major surgery after the accident. The liver had stored the anesthetics, and my body was now releasing the anesthetics that had suppressed symptoms that I should have had. So I was now experiencing those old symptoms. I was pretty impressed with both of those things. Another year or two went by, and, well, during those two years, I tried to get trained in Reiki and weird things happened. Classes canceled—they took my deposit, but like three or four times I tried to get trained and it didn't work, so I just sort of put it on the back burner.

Then I broke my ankle when I was in Costa Rica, and shortly after that, I was teaching a class that had maybe five or six people who were trained in Reiki. At the first class break, they said, "Would you like us to work on your leg?" I said, "Sure." So they put hands on and then they were chatting and talking, and I said, "Wait a minute, aren't you working on my leg?" They said, "Oh, well we can talk and still work on your leg. Reiki is about setting a healing intent. Once we've set that, the energy's channeling through us and doing the healing. We don't have to be quiet or meditate."

I went, "Oh, that's interesting." I came back and had

lunch with some veterinary friends, and one of them is a Reiki instructor, Tara Covey, DVM, and she said, "Okay, time for you to learn Reiki. What two Fridays are you available, and I'll create a class for you."

I said, "Okay," gave her the dates, she created the class, and I went to her two classes still thinking, *Oh, I'm not real good about this energy stuff. I don't know if I can do this.* Two weeks later, I was teaching one of my classes in Delaware, staying at the home of a woman who was really a dog person. She trained dogs, she trained horses, and she had a cat that I petted at about 11:00 at night after having taught all day and gone to dinner—and this cat was matted from head to tail.

I was like, "Oh." She was so embarrassed. She said, "I hoped you wouldn't see the cat. I've been trying to clip it but she just will not let me." I said, "Oh, let me do it." She had the scissors, and I worked on that cat for about half an hour. I was three snips from finishing the cat, and the cat said, "I've had it." I said, "Oh, just hang in there. I've got two snips." The piece started to fall off as the cat nailed me—claws in the back of both of my hands—and then as I was extricating from the claws, the cat bit me in the cuticle. I knew that the nail injury would take seven to 10 days to heal. Cuticle bites usually take two to three weeks to heal. I did Reiki that night. The next morning, my hands where the claws had gone in were one hundred percent healed—couldn't even tell there had been anything happening.

My finger with the cuticle bite was worse, so I taught with my finger sticking in the air or soaking in calendula tincture or holding it and doing Reiki on it all day long. By the second day, about a quarter of a teaspoon of pus came out from that little teeny spot. *Pus doesn't develop that fast*, I said to myself.

I tell everybody about SARA and about how it works with the emotions of animals and I keep emphasizing through my stories, this is something that's 100% safe.

Then it was healed. So I was sold on Reiki. From that time on, I have become a profound proponent of every single person in the world learning Reiki every time I talk to people about what they can do for their animals.

For 35 years, I was a telephone consulting homeopathic vet with some hands-on work, and for the last two years, I've been coaching people on what they can do to help their animals. Reiki is one hundred percent safe and Reiki is always the top of my list. Reiki trainings are readily available. If they've been trained how to do it with people, they can do calls with Kathleen [Prasad] about working with animals—I tell everybody about SARA and about how Reiki works with the emotions of animals. I keep emphasizing through my stories that this is something that's completely safe. Everybody should be doing it.

I really encourage everybody to offer Reiki to their entire house, to all the living beings in their house because some people have five or six animals, and they go, "Well, I can't do Reiki on each one." I say, "You don't need to. Simply offer Reiki." Sit down for 10 minutes, 15, 20, 30 minutes—whatever feels right to you, whatever you can do.

Offer the Reiki every day as the best prevention you can do for health problems. If your animals come over and want you to touch them, definitely do that. I tell a story to people that may have come from you, Kathleen. The woman, who had just had her training in Reiki, went to the barn to work on her horse. She was sure it was a shoulder problem on this horse. So she started, put her hands up, and all of a sudden the horse's skin started rippling. She went, "This is weird. What's happening?" She just went with it, and it moved her hands back to his hip and then the rippling stopped. Then she Reiki-ed the hip, realizing the problem of the lameness wasn't up front. It was in the back. The horse then got better. So I encourage people to really just allow whatever happens to happen. If people's animals leave the room, still offer it. Maybe for that day it was just too strong for them.

When I teach, Reiki is definitely one of the major protocols I recommend people use for their animals along with acupressure, flower essences, and massage because these are all one hundred percent safe. I do let people know about the other really powerful energy healing modalities like THETA touch, quantum touch, healing touch for animals, re-connective therapy, but those are not as readily available for people to find, as Reiki is, or to be trained in.

Besides, Reiki offers something that I don't think the others do as much, which is to take the bad out of things. I know that's not quite accurate. That's how I say it and sometimes I say it better! It shifts the vibration of anything you're going to be giving yourself or your animals to be more in tune with the recipient's vibrations. So if you're choosing to do heartworm preventative medicine for an animal, you can Reiki the dose before you give it. Have somebody do Reiki on the refrigerator and all the medicine dispensing areas in the office. If you are in an office where the staff is not trained in Reiki and you are, make sure to take a moment before the veterinarian goes in to see your animal to set the Reiki intent, which is healing for the highest good.

When your animal gets its legally required rabies vaccine —and only do it when your animal is well—Reiki the syringe first, then Reiki the injection site, then offer Reiki as you've been doing for as long as it's needed. If you're not yet trained in Reiki and your animal needs to get a vaccine of some sort, make sure you have a Reiki practitioner at least offering the Reiki afterwards for a few weeks in addition to some of the other holistic things that I might suggest in my practice.

When you do Reiki for your animals, the office staff will find that the animals are much easier to work with, that they recover faster from surgery, and that they may be able to help even specific problems—not necessarily always, but often. Plus an added benefit about being trained in Reiki as a veterinary office staff member is that even if your intent as the veterinarian or veterinary technician is to have the animal be as calm as possible and be as receptive as possible to the work you need to do with it, by setting that intent you're helping the people as well.

These examples are some of the reasons that I feel that every veterinary clinic should have people trained in Reiki. And I do not limit that reasoning to only animal clinics. I also think that Reiki should be used in medical centers and hospitals. I live in Baltimore and for the last, I think, eight to 10 years, the Maryland Shock Trauma Unit, which is really world famous, has all their staff trained in Reiki, and the Reiki is used both for the patients and the families because they've found there's a request for that. Many hospitals offer Reiki—a small town north of me in Pennsylvania—York, Pennsylvania—has at least two hospitals where the nurses are trained in Reiki.

If a veterinarian encourages people to learn Reiki, maybe by even offering classes in the clinic, then the people will be offering it to all living beings in their house, which means people too. So if the people are contributing to the illness of the animals, which often happens, they're going to be getting better and the relationship will be getting better and the animals will be getting better. It really is doing a universal healing. If they're feeling like the Reiki that *they* are doing is maybe helping, but they aren't sure how much, I also encourage people to consult a Reiki Master either locally or from elsewhere if their animals are really ill, and they haven't reached a place in their own experience with Reiki where they feel comfortable about it. Sometimes healing our animals can be a bit of a challenge, so if they're really ill I would add a Reiki practitioner onto the healing team. So, does that all make sense?

SARA: It does. Now, Dr. Chambreau, at your clinic, do you have Reiki practitioners who come in or are all your staff trained in Reiki?

Dr. Chambreau: I actually do not have a clinic. When I practiced as a veterinarian, I was doing telephone consulting, and that was really all I did. If local people wanted to see me in-person, we sat on the lawn or sat in my living room. So it was just me doing the Reiki. Then as I said, two years ago, I shifted to doing pet health coaching so I was no longer even being the vet prescribing the homeopathy, but more coaching the owners. I consider myself—my place on earth—to be an educator and to teach people. I was the one that helped Gail Pope get started on the holistic path with the BrightHaven animal sanctuary.[2] So teaching has been my main thing.

However, there *are* vets who offer Reiki. There is a veterinarian here in Baltimore who does do Reiki all the time, and I think his staff is trained that way. And you can also

---

2. Gail Pope, along with her husband Richard Pope, are founders of BrightHaven Center for Animal Rescue, Hospice and Holistic Education. For more information see www.brighthaven.org.

use Reiki yourself along with finding a veterinarian who offers it. I wrote a book called *The Healthy Animal's Journal*[3] that teaches people how to track their animals' symptoms, even the little, tiny ones, the early warning signs of internal imbalance—like goop in the corner of the eyes or a stinky dog. Every evaluation, weekly is best, also includes what we call at The Holistic Actions! Academy the BEAM symptoms: Behavior, Energy, Appetite, Mood, which reflect overall quality of life.

If people would use this journal, they'd be able to catch things really early. And if they were doing Reiki, they would get a sense of where something was off in a part of the body. Yet still, many practitioners, many clients don't buy the journal and don't do Reiki. So one of the challenges is what you all at SARA are addressing, which is how can we continue to inspire people who've never heard about this or who just haven't made the time in their busy lives to take this on. How can we show that this is so valuable that you need to be doing it in your veterinary practice, you need to be doing it in your barn? Imagine if everybody who had a horse barn had at least one or two people who just routinely did Reiki on all the horses in the barn? It should be worth getting fifty percent off or even free board for your horse if you did Reiki on a regular basis.

If you have a kennel, pay one of the kennel help to take the training—or even two or three of them so you would have one there at all times. That's going to decrease the diarrhea from stress in the same way giving a probiotic would decrease diarrhea from stress. In light of all these possibilities, I don't know the answer as to why other people aren't doing it.

---

3. See Dr. Chambreau's bio at the end of this chapter.

SARA: A lot of the members of SARA, the Shelter Animal Reiki Association, try to figure out the best way to approach a veterinary clinic and say, "Hey, I offer Reiki," in order to get their foot in the door. As an Animal Reiki practitioner, would you have any advice for how to approach a vet or a vet clinic?

Dr. Chambreau: Yup, I absolutely have some ideas. But first, what have they told you happens—that they don't even get to see the veterinarian or the veterinarian just says, "That sounds weird. I don't want that".

Okay. First you want to start with a veterinarian who you're working with for your own animal, whether it's a holistic veterinarian or a conventional veterinarian. So that's number one. With those people, offer to take them out to lunch. This gets them out of the veterinary clinic. They're no longer thinking *Oh, I really ought to be cleaning. Oh, I wonder if that emergency came in. Oh, how's that dog coming from surgery?*

They're out with you to lunch or dinner or breakfast or a snack or tea or a picnic—or go for a walk or a hike or whatever. You've gotten to know your vet so you want to know what it is that he or she does. Get them out of the clinic to talk to them about it.

So that's number one. Offer them something that would be enticing for them. That would work also in clinics that are small and have one veterinarian and one or two staff. Usually you can get to talk to the veterinarian there. In other clinics, you have a couple of options. Rather than going directly to the veterinarian, find out if there's an office manager and ask to speak to the office manager. They're supposed to talk to anybody who wants to talk to them. They're the filter and you do your presentation to them.

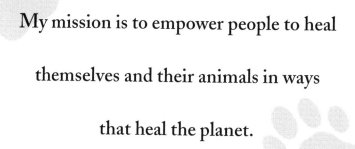

My mission is to empower people to heal themselves and their animals in ways that heal the planet.

As with any job interview, you need to do your research. You don't just come in and say, "Oh, I do Reiki. I can really help your animals. Would you like to hire me?" You know? That's not going to work. You need to find out what is missing in that clinic, what are their challenges, and that can be difficult. You can start by asking those questions. For instance, say something like, "I'd like to meet with the office manager." What about? "Well, I think I may have a solution for some of the problems that are common in many clinics, and so I'd like to have a meeting with the manager to talk about that." Again, maybe take the office manager out to lunch for the same reasons we talked about for the vet. Then ask, "What are your problems? What are some of your major issues?"

Then have some research with you. Find out about hospitals in that town that are training their nurses with Reiki. Use those. Here, I would refer to the Baltimore Shock Trauma Unit—any hard facts you can have. There are some really good books on Reiki with some research stuff in it, so that could be used, an excerpt from one. Have specific information. Then say something like, "If you have any interest at all ..." and then talk about Reiki in a more detailed way, still keeping it simple.

Say they say, "Well, one of our problems is people don't come back for follow-up visits" or "We have some stress among the technicians in the clinic"—something like that. You say, "Well, Reiki for animals is the same thing as Reiki for people. It works wonderfully for emotions with animals and it works just as well with people, so you may find that by me coming in or your staff getting trained, that could really help that issue."

Try to be as specific as you can. The other thing that just

popped into my mind since you're speaking about SARA—if you're working at a shelter, who is the veterinarian for the shelter? Is there more than one? Document. Have the people running the shelter be able to give you documentation. Ever since we've had Reiki at shelters (and I know I've seen this on the SARA website), we have an increase in adopt-ability, et cetera. Again, always when you're selling something, the important thing is to find out what the other person needs and wants.

Sometimes it can be a challenge to find out these things. It's one that I always have when I'm speaking to veterinarians, but also when I'm speaking to general pet owners. We all want our animals to live as long as possible. However, we're often frustrated by what we're told by any one approach. We may not like what the acupuncturist says to us. We may not like what the conventional vet says. When the homeopathic vet says, "Well, I really don't want you doing acupuncture at the same time because it makes it hard to evaluate," you may not be happy with that answer. So it's very frustrating. That's why I'm so excited about The Holistic Actions! Academy's help for this. Dr. Jeff Feinman has created something called the Holistic Medical Decision Making Process, HMDM.[4] It's a way to really empower people to take charge, to set a goal. I find this is important with doing Reiki as well. Set the goal. Is it to either immediately get rid of the current symptoms or to build health in a way that the body naturally gets rid of the symptoms? Reiki does both, but setting one or the other of these the goal ahead of time helps you keep going because maybe the symptom goes away, maybe the vomiting goes away quickly, but you still have a stinky dog or a cat who hides a lot.

---

4. https://www.holisticactions.com/online-courses/

If you set your goal for maximizing health, then you'll be more likely to continue doing Reiki. The Holistic Actions! Academy offers many online courses.

I face the same issues that you do when you go to a vet clinic wanting to offer Reiki. So that is what these classes will address. I know that if people come to the classes, there's going to be huge benefits for them in having more information to offer the people making the decisions to offer Reiki there.

When you go to a clinic offering Reiki, *you* know what wonderful benefits there will be for the animals, their owners, and the office or shelter staff, so it's a matter of working with the language so that you can find out what it is they need to hear. I guess the last thing, because I just am saying it for myself, is never give up and always keep trying different approaches and collecting data. That really is very important.

SARA: That's wonderful. Thank you so much for all of those great ideas. You're doing so much good for so many people with their animals and you've been doing it for over 37 years. It's pretty incredible.

Dr. Chambreau: It's great and I've just seen so much improvement. I really want to remind people that every time you take a step to use alternative modalities, you're helping the planet as well. Reiki is a perfect example of this. If you have a dog with diarrhea and you go to a conventional veterinarian, you're going to come home with some drugs. Those drugs, when administered, may stop the diarrhea, but they're going to come out in the stools. Then you'll have extra pills left over that may go in the trash, and they came in a plastic bottle and they had to be manufactured somewhere and shipped and repackaged and then shipped again. There's a big environmental footprint from that drug to stop the diarrhea. If you use slippery elm or marshmallow root, slippery elm might result in elm trees being cut down, and the marshmallow root still has to be harvested, dried, and packaged—unless you grow your own marshmallow root. Then it doesn't cost a whole lot to the environment.

Reiki is zero cost to the environment once you have your training. Yes, you have to drive to get the training or whatever. Maybe you do it online, but there's only a small cost to the environment, and then for the rest of your life, you have a way to help heal that helps the environment. Having said that, it reminds me that at one point a Reiki Master was offering Reiki, and Mother Earth said, "Hey, how come you never offer it to me?"

Make a point sometimes, every time, whatever works for you, to remember to Reiki Mother Earth, to offer Reiki to the waters, to offer Reiki to the sky and the clouds and to live as one with nature.

DR. CHRISTINA CHAMBREAU is a homeopathic veterinarian with over 37 years of experience with holistic health practices for animals and people. She began working in veterinarian clinics at the age of 11 while living on a military base in Japan. This early experience with medicine and animals led to her degree from the University of Georgia College of Veterinary Medicine in 1980. She was first introduced to homeopathy by a client at the veterinary clinic and by 1987, she was using homeopathy exclusively for her animal clients and as an advisor in phone consultations. Her interest in Reiki began with a personal experience in 1990. Her training in Reiki soon followed. Currently, Dr. Chambreau coaches people on how to care for their animals and is a speaker and lecturer on the environment, holistic health approaches for people and animals, sustainability, happiness, and success. She is also a raw food proponent for pets and people.

Dr. Chambreau adds: "My mission is to empower people to heal themselves and their animals in ways that heal the planet. As a homeopathic veterinarian, holistic health counselor, and speaker at conferences and classes all over the world, I am blessed to have my passions be my work. My wonderful husband supports me and loves me unconditionally. My daughter is my guru and my trainer. In addition to my work with homeopathy and Reiki, I am also an Awakening the Dreamer, Changing the Dream facilitator through the Pachamama Alliance. I also am a fundraiser and lead workshops for The Hunger Project. Life is Grand!"

Dr. Chambreau is the author of *Healthy Animal's Journal* and a co-author of *A Homeopathic Tutorial* and *How to Have a Stress Free Wedding and Live Happily Ever After.* She has also written two e-books for *The Healthy Dog Journal* and *The Healthy Cat Journal,* which are soon to be available, as well as a currently available e-book, co-authored by Dr. Joyce Harmon, entitled *The Healthy Horse Journal.* Please see the Resources section at the back of this book for more information about her publications.

You may contact Dr. Chambreau through her website at http://christinachambreau.com/

There is absolutely nothing that

is going to hold a match to the ability

to heal that Reiki is.

Patricia Jordan, DVM

NORTH CAROLINA

Dr. Patricia Jordan has been a practicing veterinarian since 1986. She learned about holistic healing in 2000 and was one of the first to offer Chinese veterinary practices to her animal clients. Since then she has added an extraordinarily wide range of holistic practices, including Reiki, which she learned in 2005 and consistently uses in her practice with wonderful results.

SARA: Patricia, I met you many years ago, when you took Animal Reiki classes with me, when I was first beginning to teach. Actually, I believe that Dakota, my dog at that time, was one of your teachers.

Dr. Jordan: I remember, Kathleen.

SARA: For me, that's really special to remember: that Dakota was part of your Reiki journey as well. You have been a veterinarian for many years and have so much experience in all different modalities—holistic modalities. I think it's so awesome that Reiki is a part of what you do. I'd love you to begin by telling us about yourself, your journey, and how you got to this point as a holistic vet who practices Reiki. I think that people will be very inspired when they hear your story.

Dr. Jordan: Okay. Well, there's no such thing as a short bio for me. I have been practicing veterinary medicine for 34 years. My CV is 40 pages long! I'm a constant learner. Just suffice it to say that when I went natural, I went big. Physics and energy manipulation were the source of our existence. I embraced as many of the healing modalities based in energetics as I possibly could, and I continue to do so to this very day.

SARA: Can you tell us a little bit about your first experience with holistic or alternative healing, and how it affected you?

Dr. Jordan: As far as my practice, early on, I was anchoring my practice in nutrition. So coming from the conventional form as I was, at least I had that. Nutrition is the foundation of health, and I think it keeps most of the problems at bay. But from the start, my very first experiences with healing had to do with the energetics that I employed as a child, nursing orphaned and injured wildlife. I was very, very much the neighborhood nurse for any wounded animals. Also, I don't know, I seemed to have a heat-seeking missile for animals that needed help. When you're sick, when you have nothing to work with but your hands and your heart and prayer, and your intentions, you learn very early that healing can come from the heart when you ask for it for the benefit of the patient. Coming from a place of only wanting to help is probably the most solid origin I can say that I've had in all of my healing settings.

When I found my way to Reiki, I knew when I met you, Kathleen, that you were the real deal. It just resonated so bright that I said, "Okay." Besides Dakota being a part of my path, so was BrightHaven because that's where I took Reiki I. You were so generous to allow me to do Reiki II in your hometown, because that's the other side of the country over there.

Let me talk about the very first case that I had after I finished my second Reiki class with you. I also had just left my third installment training at Healing Oasis[5] for spinal manipulation or what we call veterinary chiropractic. I've got lots of cases that stand out when Reiki was employed to help, but Ribs—he was such an amazing case. What I employed in that case was Reiki, cranial sacral, and, then also, the spinal manipulation.

After your class, I went to Arizona to have a chance to work with RAV, which is the Remote Area Veterinary Services. It's serving underserved populations in the United States. This one was in White River, the Apache reservation in Arizona. There was a pit bull there, and he was so severely emaciated. That's why his nickname was Ribs. He was in terrible shape because people had used him as a bait dog in pit bull fighting rings. He was full of tubes. He had drains all coming out of his sides. He was on constant IV antibiotics and painkillers. The look on his face was one that I'll never forget. It was like he had lost

---

5. https://healingoasis.edu/

his soul, like he had no life fire, no desire to live. He was a rescue from the service position that they had previously had before the reservation they were then on. No one had claimed him, and so they were just caring for him, doing the best they could.

The veterinarian in charge showed me his x-rays. He clearly had an identifiable atlanto-occipital subluxation (AOS)[6] at the very top of his head. This is probably the worst horror that any chiropractic student could run into because it's one of the worst types of injuries. The only thing worse would be an internal decapitation because of a full dislocation. I was fearful to attempt to even try to fix this, and I was so green. I was green in everything—including Reiki. Even well-trained and experienced chiropractors can actually end up entrapping an artery in this area, in a way that can result in death for humans and so also for animals. I felt like I didn't have the training to handle the case. When I told this to the veterinarian in charge, he said to me, "I want to let you know, I don't have to worry about what happens to him because he doesn't have an owner. It's okay because if he doesn't make it, it's okay." I was horrified by that statement. But anyway, I went over there to visit him in his cage. The cage door was open because he wasn't going anywhere. He was lying there with the tubes hanging out. He was so

---

6. AOD is a highly unstable craniocervical injury, resulting from damage to ligaments and/or bony structures connecting the skull to the cervical spine. It is historically associated with significant neurological morbidity and mortality secondary to brainstem and upper cervical spinal cord injury. Although AOD represents roughly only 1% of all cervical spine injuries in the acute care setting, it has been reported to be the most common cervical spine injury in motor vehicle accident (MVA) fatalities. Modern case reports, however, have documented improved neurological outcomes, likely as a result of earlier diagnosis and surgical stabilization. https://www.ncbi.nlm.nih.gov/pmc/articles/PMC4363805/

sad-looking. Like I said, he just didn't look like he had any hope or joy.

I proceeded to engage with what was left of his spirit. I asked permission to treat with Reiki. I also used cranial sacral. I laid hands on him over those areas that were so damaged, but without ever coming close enough to even do a manipulation. Instead, I used my prayer and intention and called on Reiki. I also visualized with cranial sacral. Surprisingly, he allowed me to engage for 45 minutes in a slow and steady intentional healing for his highest good, and also for the retrieval of his soul, for forgiveness for what had happened to him. My heart was truly pumping out endorphins for him. I could feel it.

He didn't really show me any change except the one that we are so grateful for, which is that he fell asleep. He fell into a really, really deep sleep. For the first time, he actually appeared to be at rest. When I was done, I thanked the universe. I thanked everyone whose prayers and intentions for this dog had been positive. I collected every positive unclaimed prayer for his highest good. I was really worried about him, because that night, he just didn't look like he had any will to live. But the next morning there was a phenomenal change. I saw him standing past the cages. He was wagging his tail. He was looking very bright-eyed; he looked like he had his life fire back.

I went to him, and he actually shoved his head into my overturned hand, even before I was able to ask him for permission. You can't really order up a healing like that. It was just amazing to me that everything in this dog had shifted. It was a 180 degree turn around. I was happy to engage him for another session. It was much shorter, and it was stronger and from a different kind of direction. I felt like he was a participant, actively, in that energy.

I think that Reiki is a place where they can actually extend their own heart's desire to be doing the right thing and to be making it work, not only for themselves, as a practiced way of life, but for their patients, which is the reason we're supposed to be in this.

I left him to go work with my student surgeons that day. I was the only woman veterinarian leading a surgery team for spays and neuters for these animals on this reservation. At lunch time, I had a little break, and I went to where Ribs had been. I didn't see him there. The veterinarian in charge told me, "Hey, I have good news. Someone's willing to give Ribs a home. They've come forward, and he now has a caretaker. The drains have all been taken out." He was doing fantastic, and he was even slated to go to a new home the next day. This was as close to a miracle as you ever, ever see—what Reiki had done for this patient. I feel like that part of it was also him getting a home, getting a place to go. It reignited his life fire.

Moreover, I feel like it corrected his near-decapitation. We had x-rays to show that that definitely had been his problem. Everything was better, even his heart. You just can't accomplish this type of healing with anything, I don't think, other than Reiki. I also shared this case when I got back to my next session at Healing Oasis. Truthfully, I was actually afraid to. I was the last one to chime in with a response to "what's new since last time we saw you?" I told them. I said, "I did not do a physical manipulation on that dog's head, but apparently, between the cranial sacral visualization and running some Reiki, it actually happened." After this small pause, they admitted to me that they'd heard other stories like mine—that it was definitely possible.

Looking at the reason for Ribs having made a good response just shows me how strong the spirit of Reiki fire is. This story is one of many that has been made available in the *American Holistic Veterinary Medical Association Journal* (AHVMA).[7] It's one that I'm sure that a lot of people

---

7. https://www.ahvma.org/ahvma-journal/

have run into and maybe has made the difference for people understanding what Reiki is. It's just, to me, amazing. There is absolutely nothing that is going to hold a candle to the ability to heal that Reiki has.

SARA: How did everyone else around you react to that—to Ribs recovery? What was the general response? Did people support Reiki during that time? I'm really curious to know if people even acknowledged that it could have been Reiki that created this amazing recovery.

Dr. Jordan: We didn't know. When I talked to the veterinarian in charge, specifically, he was very interested in the fact that I had been training at Healing Oasis and had chiropractic training, so I could do spinal manipulation. They didn't know anything about Reiki, and I don't really remember even sharing that. I, as an early practitioner, was struggling. I felt like I couldn't lead a class in teaching it. I was still learning myself. But we were all very busy in the project that we had going, so I guess, maybe, only I understood where the shift had come from, the energy shift that happened just within that dog alone. You could tell because he made the choice the next morning to run up underneath my hand, so he understood where the healing had come from.

I can't say that this was a great teaching moment for the entire group. They were calling me Dr. Good Drugs because I am also an herbalist, and I was running health food and nutrition to everybody. The subject of Reiki wasn't really broached during that time, but *I* knew where it had come from. The other people were mainly really just glad that the dog was doing so much better. I don't think anybody really was there to witness how much of a miracle it was. As for the veterinarian in charge, I didn't even go over it with him. He saw me go over there and work on him, but he didn't make the connection.

SARA: I think that's the experience of a lot of practitioners who work in shelters and other situations. They see, and the animals understand, but there may not be a wider understanding of what has happened. That's okay because the animals understand. And we're there for the animals anyway, right?

Dr. Jordan: Right, and the important one is the one that benefited. That was my first case. I have other cases that I was involved with during which surely the other veterinarians in the area knew exactly what it was that I was doing. Oh, this was a goat, this other patient, who had been hit by an 18-wheeler. The goat had been brought into the hospital on emergency, and I feel, wrongly taken in and administered steroid when the animal was in obvious pain and stress and was unlikely to survive due to the severed spinal cord. Taking in a case like that, knowingly generating revenue and extending the suffering of the animal for profit, was wrong for the veterinarian to do.

I was very concerned because I saw the x-rays. There was a huge defect within the spinal cord where it had snapped. I believed this animal was not going to make a recovery. I thought it was in pain, and I thought it was absolutely cruel that he was even being kept alive at all. The owner came in, and I took her back there to visit him. She looked right at me, and she was really concerned and upset. She said, "This doesn't look good. I don't think he's going to make it." I knew that he wasn't going to make it either, so I asked her for permission to do Reiki.

    I laid my hands on him as I did the Reiki. He was in such a painful and terrorized state that I can't say that permission was granted or there was anything other than panic. That goat passed almost immediately, as soon as I had put hands on him, before I could go through the formalities, the way that I was taught by you, Kathleen. I really feel like it went so fast that it was just exactly what the goat wanted. I think, Kathleen, if you'll remember, maybe a year or two later, there was a telephone conference that you had with other Reiki members, and we discussed the fact that sometimes the highest good means that they quickly pass.

    Anyway, that was the second case that I had done at that hospital. The first one was a little Bijon puppy. That puppy was so drawn to me for some reason. He came in with a collapsed lung. We have x-rays to prove that. Because that puppy was so drawn to me, he just wouldn't stop staring at me. Even while I was in the hospital having to multi-task with other patients, I had that connection with him. I ran Reiki, and I did all of the exact same things that I would do if I was solely working on that patient, without the other distractions of all these other patients that I had to work with. His lung re-inflated, and we had post-x-rays to prove that as well. This case was also one that was written up for the *AHVMA Journal* and possibly in one of your online columns, Kathleen.

    In this hospital, the doctors knew about energy work. Most of those veterinarians were from South America, so

I feel like they already had an understanding that, yes, this kind of energy work could definitely work, but they were conventional to the bone. They were just, like, "You can do the Reiki," but they didn't understand how to charge for it or whatever. So, it became my goal to try to at least open their eyes to the possibility that, hey, you could actually lay a foundation for your practice with this. That never went over there, at that practice, but I certainly have incorporated Reiki into mine.

SARA: These are amazing stories. The fact that you're able to have these x-rays to document how Reiki helped adds so much because that is not often the case. Can you talk a little bit about your practice and the modalities that you offer, as well as how you incorporate Reiki into your practice?

Dr. Jordan: Sure. I probably have more holistic modalities or energy modalities than any other practitioner in the United States and, possibly, the world! The list is very extensive. As far as Reiki, however, I always underpin my life, the foundation for my practice, and how I even try to face the world each day with the principles that I've learned that are important to Reiki and by following the ethics and the Five Precepts that I learned from you, Kathleen. I feel like, as far as every time, every minute of every day, I try to incorporate what I've learned about the benefits of universal healing for the highest good in every way possible.

My first major study was with traditional Chinese veterinary medicine, and I was one of the first practitioners in the United States. I use acupuncture, herbal medicine, food therapy, Tui-Na,[8] Amma,[9] which is a type of soft tissue manipulation. I do post-diagnosis work with the Norwegian veterinarian Are Thoreson[10] and have also incorporated spinal manipulation from Healing Oasis, cranial sacral, and dousing and subtle-energy work. I learned these last two fields from third-generation Scottish energy workers. I'm not sure exactly what that means, but there are a lot of energy workers that come from Scotland. I studied homeopathy under Dr. Richard Pitcairn[11] and some others, but I also learned quantum touch,[12] emotional freedom techniques (EFT),[13] and have done a little bit with vortex healing.[14] I am certified in Nambudripad's Allergy Elimination Techniques (NAET).[15]

---

8. "*Tuina* (pronounced "twee nah") is a form of Oriental bodywork that has been used in China for centuries. A combination of massage, acupressure and other forms of body manipulation, *tuina* works by applying pressure to acupoints, meridians and groups of muscles or nerves to remove blockages that prevent the free flow of *qi*. Removing these blockages restores the balance of *qi* in the body, leading to improved health and vitality." www.acupuncturetoday.com/abc/tuina.php

9. "Amma is a specialized form of touch therapy that combines deep tissue manipulation with pressure, friction massage and touch to specific acupuncture points, along with various muscles, ligaments, joints and tendinomuscular junctions. Translated literally, amma means "push-pull." As with acupuncture, the goals of amma are to remove blockages, ease stress and promote the circulation of *qi*, which helps restore and maintain health. Most amma practitioners also receive extensive training in nutrition and dietary advice." www.easttowesttherapies.com/types-of-asian-bodywork.html

10. www.bevas.eu/en/are_thoresen

11. www.drpitcairn.com/

12. https://www.quantumtouch.com/en/?option=com_content&view=article&id=3

13. nickortner.com

14. https://www.vortexhealing.org/

15. www.naet.com/about/what-is-naet/

I do prolotherapy,[16] and all manner of herbal medicine—Western, Chinese, and Ayurvedic. I've also delved into and become certified in crystal and stone medicine, which for me is actually a very good partnership with Reiki.

I consider myself a planetary herbalist. I study herbs used throughout the world, including from the shamans' perspective and from our teacher, Earth. Currently, I'm fascinated by the information from healers who have found that in teaching plant ceremonies, there are plant allies that can manifest the medicine that we need, even if the plant we're working with is not one that has possession of the exact constituents that we need. I've really opened up my eyes to the many things that this world encompasses.

I have three years of naturopathic recipes on the burner, and I'm currently working on three books about this area of my practice. The title of one book will be *Back to the Garden*. I also have a natural rearing template for animals that mirrors the natural living rearing that we need to employ for ourselves. This book will be called *Natural Healthy Living*. Then, also, I am working on a 911 emergency first aid, disaster, and acute remedy book using homeopathy, as it seems to be what we need in the near future here. In fact, my clients have said, "Can you move that one up to the first book you finish?"

---

16. "Prolotherapy (Proliferative Therapy), also known as Non-Surgical Ligament and Tendon Reconstruction and Regenerative Joint Injection, is a recognized orthopedic procedure that stimulates the body's healing processes to strengthen and repair injured and painful joints and connective tissue. It is based on the fact that when ligaments or tendons (connective tissue) are stretched or torn, the joint they are holding destabilizes and can become painful. Prolotherapy, with its unique ability to directly address the cause of the instability, can repair the weakened sites and produce new collagen tissue, resulting in permanent stabilization of the joint. Once the joint is stabilized, pain usually resolves." prolotherapycollege.org/what-is-prolotherapy/

SARA: I know that you are also one of the world's experts in vaccinosis.[17] Your book, *Mark of the Beast: Hidden in Plain Sight*[18] explains your views on this subject.

Dr. Jordan: Yes, and it's not only about the vaccine damage to the animals, but also to us as humans. That book, I really feel, was channeled. At the time, I had just covered 700 cases in three months of direct vaccine-induced disease. I was telling my colleague that another one of my colleagues had sent me a 35-page paper written by Canadian naturopath Dr. André Saine[19] on vaccine damage, and that it was more definitive evidence of what I had written on the subject and what others had written before me.

What I would like to say about this is that I've always been interested in nutrition and the understanding that food is information to the body. However, going through veterinary school, I had no idea that vaccinations were critical-nutrient-depleting—Vitamin C depletion is one example of this. As a matter of fact, all of the drugs that we use deplete the body in at least one critical nutrient. The adverse effects that you see from both of these—whether you're talking about biologically derived medicines, like vaccines, or chemically derived pharmaceuticals—have to do with the critical-nutrient deficiencies that they're creating.

As my exploration of energy matter has expanded with the many modalities that I have studied, I feel like I've finally started to see the connection of source with that tiniest light particle that actually is energy. This is how I'm trying to

---

17. dr-jordan.com/?s=vaccinosis

18. Ibid.

19. www.homeopathy.ca/about-us/andre-saine-d-c-n-d-f-c-a-h/

understand now how to fix what we've damaged. I'll just say this about Reiki, in particular. One of my colleagues believes that you can still vaccinate, but just do Reiki and it won't matter. I said, "That's absolutely not true." Everything that's getting vaccinated is getting damaged. I think the message is very clear to us that we have to stop doing that because it's actually causing genetic damage. The highest good isn't to pretend that this isn't our lesson to learn.

SARA: You have brought up something else interesting that I would like to explore with you. You've just spoken a little bit about how you believe that people, like the animals that you treat, respond negatively to vaccines, so there are similarities between animals and people's responses to certain agents. You've talked to me before about how animals and people can mirror each other's diseases, for instance when an animal comes to you with a specific disease and then the animal's caretaker might also manifest the same symptoms or maybe even have that exact same disease. I know that you've seen that quite a lot. Can you talk a little bit about that and how you might handle that in the context of Reiki? Do you ever include people in an Animal Reiki session? Do you talk to people about their own healing? How does that work?

Dr. Jordan: That can be a real prickly step because some people don't believe you have any business bringing that up. I have an e-book on my website that has to do with emotions and how emotions are directed energy.[20] What I've come to learn is that the emotions are a type of directional energy. As far as our animals are concerned, there are other

---

20. *Emotions and Biological Harmony in Humans and Pets.* See www.dr-jordan.com/

members of AHVMA who also have come to the realization that where an animal has been in the caretaker's home for a good amount of its life, somehow the human's ethereal health is being entrained to be the same as the client's.

Right now, I can tell you what's happening because I was talking about this just this morning, and this is exciting. I was listening to an MD who was one of the speakers about emotional freedom techniques at Nick and Jessica Ortner's Tapping Summit[21] this summer. She realized that if you are in sympathetic overdrive, so you're very, very, very anxious and you're in that fight or flight mode, what happens to the body is that this state of being prevents the body from being in the healing mode. When I heard her say that, I said, "That's it!" That is how these animals are being affected by their owner's sympathetic overdrive.

I don't want anyone to feel guilty because these things that happen with our emotions or our instincts have been set up to be automatic. It takes, really, a lot, I think, of education and training and perception to see that you can step into a situation where you're freaking out or you're ready to run or you're ready to fight and then see the caution light and say, "Okay, I'm going to step away from this, and I'm going to get myself out of that." There are all sorts of different ways to do this, and we need these things right now because what's happening is that while we're in this mode where we cannot heal, it's also disabling our animals from being able to heal.

This directional force that exists because of this energy can drive things to diseases like cancer and even straight into death. That's how this is all working. I was halfway excited to figure this out but at the same time realizing that a lot more

---

21. www.thetappingsolution.com/blog/tapping-world-summit-2018/

training had to be going on to try to help this situation—for both the patient and the client to redirect it. This is where I would step aside and let Reiki help—when you can't talk to people because they can't hear you because they're in this mode of fight or flight. Really, there are some things I know about that would help here, like aroma therapy, where you can actually get a fast response with scent. But there are a lot of times when we can witness what's happening and we can't do a darn thing about it except offer Reiki.

I've talked to some other friends of mine and practitioners and said, "Isn't it sad that we don't remember that this is the first thing that we should be doing?" The first thing we should be employing is Reiki and prayer rather than coming to these as a last resort. I think we could learn how powerful Reiki can be for this, but I have seen this state of fight or flight in others, and I've been there myself, so I know how absolutely scary and how unhearing you can be, how deaf you can be to the situation. Then it really becomes the need for those who have embraced the power of universal healing and what it can be and have learned to focus it. What I think is really needed is that we remember that healing is within us and that it exists only for the highest good, however that comes out, even like in the situation with the goat. Until we come up with a way to really be able to put two inches of sprung spinal cord back together, we need to accept that the highest good is sometimes—you know sometimes—it's death. Sometimes it's learning a lesson that's going to benefit the whole, not just you and the patient and the client in the room, but all of mankind, actually. I think the planet's really speaking up right now for needing that.

I personally would absolutely encourage all members of the animal health care team to learn Reiki.

SARA: Yes, absolutely. That's beautiful. You're such a philosopher, Patricia. I love that about you. Before we finish, can you speak about an issue that affects a lot of SARA members who work with shelter animals and also other animal Reiki practitioners? One of the bridges that we try to build is with the veterinary community. Do you have any advice about how to bridge that gap—how to get Reiki into a veterinary setting?

Dr. Jordan: Thinking as a veterinarian myself, I would try to get the veterinarians to understand how important Reiki is as an underpinning or foundation for their entire practice. I personally would absolutely encourage all members of the animal healthcare team to learn Reiki. It's hard to accomplish this though because in the conventional training world, talking about Reiki has no place. They want more marketing and more business management, but they're missing the boat completely.

I think the best thing to do is to use situations like my three stories for those that can think outside the box so they can hear examples of how Reiki's been so important to animals, like those that I have worked with. It will help them understand that other people can ease them into learning Reiki themselves, or at least be the Reiki presence in that practice, until more and more of it can be personally embraced by them—that they will become part of the family and that by living their lives with the foundation of Reiki, they have the prospect to be better citizens for our planet and more capable healers.

I'll tell you what—the doctorate degree does not make you a healer—not at all. Most of the healers that I know do not wear white coats. Having the right heart is a necessary start, and it's the best practice. It'll come from those that are mentored in this process, from what I consider the right direction, the right way. It comes from the heart. It's hard because when you graduate from veterinary school, you have all these bills, and you've been just brainwashed into essentially being a salesman for biologicals and drugs and processed foods—all these things that I know. But it didn't take me more than 10 years. I'm not a rocket scientist, but I saw that if you did what they said, you could just about predict the damage that was going to come in the door on the next annual visit. It really takes somebody with a strong constitution to be able to step up, get up, and walk out of church when it's not the right sermon. I think that Reiki is a place where they can actually extend their own heart's desire to be doing the right thing and to be making it work, not only for themselves, as a practiced way of life, but for their patients, which is the reason we're supposed to be in this. Right?

SARA: Yes, absolutely, Patricia. Thank you so much for all of your stories, your amazing stories and wisdom. I'm so excited that Reiki has been a part of your journey and that you've been a part of my journey.

Dr. Jordan: Thank you, Kathleen. You've had a remarkable journey yourself. I was just thinking back to when I said to my colleagues, "Hey, American Holistic Veterinary Medical Association, I think you should learn about Reiki. So why don't we have Kathleen come in and teach us." Then I did a book review for one of your books. And right after that, one person did come up to me at that conference and say, "Thank you so much because I was wondering about that."

It's the wonder that we want to cultivate, so "Good for you!" because you've brought it so far in an amazing amount of time.

SARA: A lot of it is thanks to you for really helping to support me. I really appreciate that.

Dr. Jordan: Well, like I said, as long as we have this as a family, really good things can happen.

DR. PATRICIA JORDAN is a 1986 graduate of the North Carolina College of Veterinary Medicine. Having practiced conventional veterinary medicine for fifteen years and originated four different veterinary practices in North Carolina, Dr. Jordan found holistic medicine in 2000 at the American Holistic Veterinary Medical Association (AHVMA) Conference in Williamsburg, Virginia. Until the AHVMA meeting, many, many dead ends were predictably showing up in cases treated conventionally.

Holistic medicine ignited a pathway towards many of the modalities that provided Dr. Jordan with the inspiration to follow the path of healing with energy and intention. Working to complete a Master's Program in Traditional Chinese Veterinary Medicine with Dr. Xie of the Chi Institute and participating in Dr. Richard Pitcairn's Professional Course for Veterinarians opened the way to naturopathic medicine for Dr. Jordan.

Memberships in the AHVMA, the Veterinary Botanical Medicine Association, and the Academy of Veterinary Homeopathy have also provided her with a much wider range of healing options. Dr. Jordan was a student of Kathleen Prasad for Reiki I and II. In Dr. Jordan's words, "It was this energy work that has allowed me to move past just the physical and channel healing for the non-physical, the emotional, mental, and spiritual, a communication that addresses the entire macrocosm and for the purpose of the highest good. We never learned that in conventional training!"

You may contact Dr. Jordan through her website at http://dr-jordan.com/

We set out to study the effects of Reiki treatment in the veterinarian practice. …Overall, we were very impressed with the group's response to Reiki treatments as a whole. For those technicians and others that were involved—their commitment to Reiki was solidified by that study. It was wonderful.

Marc Malek, DVM

SACRAMENTO, CALIFORNIA

Dr. Marc Malek is a veterinarian at Foothill Farms Veterinary Hospital in Sacramento, California. He is a Reiki-trained veterinarian and a member of SARA. Dr. Malek is a 1990 graduate of the UC Davis School of Veterinary Medicine. He became interested in energy medicine in 2011 and by 2014 he had transformed his traditional western practice into an integrative practice that incorporates Reiki, acupuncture, therapeutic laser, essential oils and herbal medicine.

SARA: Dr. Malek, I'd love if you could tell us a bit about yourself to begin with so our readers can have a better idea of your work and your experience. I know you are both a conventional veterinarian and a holistic veterinarian, so you use integrative medicine, which is really fascinating and wonderful. Maybe you could speak a bit about yourself and your journey up to this point.

Dr. Malek: It has been a long and interesting road, that's for sure. I graduated from UC Davis School of Veterinary Medicine in 1990, with the intention of practicing as a companion animal veterinarian focusing on horses, dogs, and cats with a real interest in surgery. During the first couple of years, I did do mixed animal practice incorporating all species and I loved it. It was a great learning experience. Traditional medicine was all I ever really was thinking about at that point in my life.

Acupuncture would pop in and out, I'd hear about it and I'd think, *"How could this possibly work—poking needles in creatures and having them respond in some healing way?"* I really didn't understand it, but eventually I thought *You know, with 5,000 plus years of practice and millions to billions of individuals who were sold on the process, there must be something to it.* However, the time that it takes to actually dedicate yourself to another whole modality is daunting when you're just trying to learn and are just beginning a veterinary practice. So although I was really interested in how acupuncture might work, my thought then was *Maybe I'll look into it someday...*

It got tabled for quite a while and ultimately it came boomeranging back in 2014, when I trained for and received my medical acupuncture certification. I was able to use acupuncture for large animals, equine, and small animals. I've been an active acupuncture practitioner for the last four years or so. Reiki had also come into my life—as a lot of these energy-based practices did, starting in 2011, although not Reiki per se in '11, but a change that converted me into a believer in spirit and a believer in energy medicine, a very personal experience that basically changed my whole life.

In 2011, after that experience, I began meditating and actually became a disciple of Paramanhansa Yogananda under Self-Realization Fellowship's correspondence program. I was initiated as a Kriya Yogi in 2014. 2014 was a big year for me. I designed and developed our new practice, became an acupuncture certified veterinarian, a Kriya Yogi and completed Shinpiden. I had already spent a year basically studying the effects of Reiki within our practice. I first got directed towards you, Kathleen, in 2013. I spent the first year really doing investigation into the value of Reiki in our practice, and it was amazing. You came up here to give, I think, about six or eight of us Reiki 1. I had a core of Reiki practitioners that were working for me. We went about trying to use it wherever we could and then studying the results. Studying from a prospective standpoint, we would have people fill out questionnaires about the quality of their pet's life after they began receiving Reiki and we did not charge them for it so we could get a better idea of how it fit in and how we might utilize it.

From there, it's been an amazing four or five years. We moved from our smaller practice space that we'd been in since '94, bought a 14,000 square foot building, and utilized about 9,000 square feet of it. This building has seven exam rooms; we used to have two. Our practice incorporates Reiki, laser therapy, acupuncture, essential oils, and we use some herbs. So it's really changed the whole complexion of our practice and the size of the practice, and it's been a success. We were doing well in our tiny building, but now that it has continued to amplify and grow, we just feel really wonderfully blessed that we're able to share what we have with Sacramento and the surrounding areas.

SARA: I wanted to ask you a bit more about this study that you did. You collected data from clients that had received Reiki. Can you share some of your findings with us?

Dr. Malek: We set out to study the effects of Reiki treatment in the veterinary practice. We had a set of questions that we would ask and have people rate their answers using a scale of one to five or one to 10 about the changes in their companion animal right after the session and what happened during that week. We'd have them fill it out weekly. We developed a questionnaire based on their animal's quality of life—various things like, "Are they able to get up better? How long can they walk? What's their appetite like on a scale of one to 10?" We went through a whole litany of questions, and they had to agree to fill that form out in order to partake in our free study.

I was really surprised at the number of people who were eager actually to participate. The patient selection, the patients that we chose to include, were those that really didn't have a good medical or surgical answer for their problems—old-age patients, cancer-type patients that weren't going to be going for chemotherapy, or degenerative diseases that would cause weakness in the rear end, for example. Old dog vestibular syndrome was one that really seemed to respond well to Reiki; it's an off-balance condition in older dogs, a stroke-like syndrome, and we got good responses with that.

Overall, we were very impressed with the groups responses to Reiki treatments as a whole. For those technicians and others that were involved—their commitment to Reiki was solidified by that study. It was wonderful.

SARA: That's awesome. How long did that study go for and how many clients were in it? How many Reiki treatments did they receive during this test?

Dr. Malek: We were doing them usually like once or twice a week. We had, I think a total of 40 or 50 that were involved. Like I said, it went on for about a year, and then we said, "Okay, well we're convinced this is working well and we're going to go ahead and offer it." Then we converted it into a paid service ... but we still offer the first two treatments at no cost because I feel it's an experiential service that clients have to experience to really understand its value for their animal. Not that I'm not confident that it works, but I think many people are somewhat skeptical, of course.

SARA: I have several more questions about this that will help our SARA members and other readers understand how they can better explain the importance of Reiki to veterinarians and to shelter personnel. How does it actually work? Do you have the people bring their animals to your clinic? What is the space like where they receive Reiki, and what does a session look like? What's the average number of treatments that most people like their animals to receive or that you recommend to them?

Dr. Malek: I'll start with the first part, which is that we have a room that we term the energy room. We do Reiki, we do acupuncture, and we do our laser treatments in there. We try to avoid doing painful procedures or things that would bring really sick, contagious animals in that space. It's more of a calm space; we have a diffuser with essential oils in there. We have it decorated in a more eastern style, with ferns and with Kanji[22] on the wall. It's a different space.

In terms of the frequency of the treatments, that really depends on the condition of the animal and the owner's ability to make the appointments, of course. In terms of the length of time, it's variable, but typically we try to aim for 20 to 30 minutes. Usually it's not me... I can explain that later. It's the technicians who are the ones that are trained that currently do the Reiki.

SARA: Do you have volunteers that come in and offer Reiki on a volunteer basis?

Dr. Malek: We have had some volunteers that have done that, sort of externs that wanted to work within our practice to see how we were functioning and to donate their time to the animals—not only the animals that were coming in for the various energy treatment sessions but also for the patients in the hospital.

SARA: That's wonderful. What advice would you give to a Reiki practitioner who would love to ally with a vet on how to do that or what qualities would you look for in that type of an external practitioner?

Dr. Malek: If I'm going to be very real about this, then I have to say that I think it's going to take the right veterinary setting.

---

22. "*Kanji* are ideograms, i.e. each character has its own meaning and corresponds to a word. By combining characters, more words can be created." https://www.japan-guide.com/e/e2046.html

I think that most Western traditional veterinary practitioners might be a bit skeptical and maybe standoffish about it. They might be resistant. I think you probably feel that as well. A vet who is more of a holistic or integrative type practitioner is going to be more receptive. However, I think that you can break into any practice with the right attitude. What do I look for? First of all, be confident in what you're approaching them with. It would be the same thing I would look for in anyone who I would want to associate with—someone who's authentic, who's compassionate, who's dedicated, who's intelligent, and honest, with basic, good qualities—good people. That doesn't mean that you have to be this stellar person to come into my practice. But if you ask what I am looking for, those would be the qualities and the potential. Feeling that dedication to animal well-being and human well-being—that's what would definitely make it for me.

SARA: Marc, how do other vets view what you're doing? Do you ever get any pushback? Or do you get other vets saying, "Oh, wow, this is a great idea, I'd love to do what you're doing." What's the general response from your peers?

Dr. Malek: I don't spend a lot of time in large groups of veterinarians. The veterinarians that I have working for me all have been through Reiki 1, because I teach Reiki 1 to my employees. They weren't all necessarily looking for Reiki, but certainly seeing how we practice it and how it goes on, they were all willing to go through Reiki 1 and at least experience that.

They're not all what I would consider to be Reiki practitioners, but they've been Reiki attuned and they're aware of what it is. Other veterinarians? I haven't really had anybody resistant that I've talked to. I think other veterinarians, after they hear that I'm doing it, go, "What the heck? What is that?" But I haven't had anybody being critical or saying, "You lost your marbles " or anything like that. Again I'm surprised by most responses. I was invited through individuals that knew of you, Kathleen, to be part of Washington State's veterinarian holistic club. They invited me up and I gave a talk. I was well-received and it was wonderful. From a veterinary student standpoint, that was great. Overall, it's been all good.

SARA: That's so awesome. Can you talk a bit about how you find the time to use Reiki in your practice and how you use it? You said that it was usually the techs who did the Reiki sessions. So how do you use it as a veterinarian?

Dr. Malek: That's a great question, and I may go on and on 'cause I'm very passionate about it! This actually goes back to you again because I always thought *How can I do a session; how can I do this? I have to prepare, I have to do X, Y, Z, and sit down.* But I learned from you that it's not that way—that ultimately I *am* Reiki, so it's not a problem.

In terms of getting there, I just take a deep breath, I feel my energy and I'm there. How do I get there? That's the practice—my meditative practice that I do every day so that I'm always in touch. It just takes that change in intention and focus to be there. When going into a surgery, right before I begin the incision, I just take a breath, and essentially say, "Let me perform this surgery for this animal's highest good." I feel the energy and I'm working.

By having everybody Reiki certified and attuned, that change that goes on within the individual is something that then as you guys know, spreads out into the field.

When I'm in an exam room, it's a very similar thing. It's actually most amazing with cats because they're on the table and I'm standing in front of them. I take my breath, I look them in the eye, I let them know through my intention that I don't want to hurt them, that I want to help them, and then I lay my hands on them and they feel my energy and they change. That's something that caregivers as well as my workers or my technicians can see. They see a difference in the animal's reaction to my interaction versus others interactions.

There are so many comments and observations about this. "How come they do so well with you? They don't do so well with us." I don't look at it as, "Oh, I'm the best at doing X." I just look at it as I'm Reiki, they feel it, and they know it, so I'm lucky and blessed to be able to express that through me.

SARA: That's beautiful. I just want to interject something here about when you were in your smaller clinic before you moved into your big one. I came to do a Reiki share there, which was really fun—to be able to do some Reiki together. While I was there, you had some clients in the waiting room, and you went out to see those people and greet some other people that were out there. I witnessed such a compassionate presence with your human clients and the patients in just the way that you were when you saw them and went over to them. It choked me up actually. I was not necessarily expecting to feel that energy, that compassion and kindness and what you exude in the space where you are. But I did and that was really incredible for me to see and feel.

Just how in SARA we want to make shelters and

sanctuaries places of peace, you don't always think of a veterinary clinic as a place of peace. But I've seen and felt that you've created that where you are. So I just wanted to share that with you and with our readers.

Dr. Malek: That's wonderful to hear, Kathleen. That really makes me feel like we're accomplishing what we set out to do, which is to really create. You've got to come see my new place because it's physically and energetically there. People mention this all the time. "Hey, the energy is just so good here." They don't necessarily know what they're saying; they're just saying, "We just feel so good when we walk in here. The animals are calm."

That's really what I wanted to do—to create that space that allows healing to magnify and for people to feel comfortable. Because it is a stressful situation often times bringing animals in who are fearful, worrying about their conditions. There's all of that. We don't need to contribute to that by being cold and an apparently uncaring place. That's completely against what we want to provide as healers.

SARA: Would you share a couple of stories of animals that have been helped with Reiki?

Dr. Malek: Sure. There have been many of them but some of them are just really near and dear to my heart. One was a dog named Nicki, and she was a mixed breed terrier, who I'd been seeing all her life. Her owner was very well-meaning and a great owner but she, herself, was very anxious and nervous and was having some medical issues. The first time I approached her about Nicki, Nicki had some rear-end weakness. I was talking about how with certain types of degenerative myelopathy[23] and neuro problems with the rear end, we don't have a really great treating modality in Western medicine. Acupuncture can be useful, but at that time I didn't use acupuncture. I was drawn to offer her Reiki for her dog because of that. Then I realized *She really needs it. She really needs Reiki for what's going on with her as well for her emotional state.* That is something that I've seen, and it's happened on a number of occasions. I can talk a little bit more about that and elaborate later.

Nicki's course was pretty miraculous. She didn't become normal, but she saw great and positive changes in her ability to move and in her attitude. She was depressed before that because she couldn't get around as well, so she improved with her movement. But she also improved with her attitude. She was more confident; she would come in before and be scared. Sometimes we even had to muzzle her because she was fearful. As a result of being at our practice as frequently as she was, receiving Reiki, and honestly, feeling the benefits as a patient, she really received the benefits.

She actually began looking forward to coming in to have these treatments once or twice a week. She ultimately got so well that her owner stopped bringing her because she was feeling so well. Then she had another issue, that old dog vestibular syndrome, when they have a stroke-like phenomenon where they become very off-balance. It does self-correct over time but they're usually left with some physical deficits—head tilt, some off-balance nature, and what not.

Normally they respond over a period of a couple weeks.

---

23. Myelopathy is a disorder that results from severe compression of the spinal cord. https://www.hopkinsmedicine.org/healthlibrary/conditions/nervous_system_disorders/myelopathy_22,Myelopathy

They get better, fairly well, they stop falling as much in the first few days. Then after a couple weeks, usually they're doing better, well enough to get around. But this was one of the more miraculous cases when she came in and started having Reiki. She was completely better in a week.

Obviously, we can't say with one hundred percent certainty that she wouldn't have recovered well. My intuitive sense knows that the Reiki treatments, as it helped her in the past, were really what helped catalyze her healing here. That was wonderful and a good success story.

Two more parts of this story are near and dear to my heart. One is that ultimately, when she ended up failing towards the end of her life, she came in for an end of life care in Reiki. Her last day when we had to say goodbye, she was receiving Reiki from three people. Her transition was beautiful, it was amazing. That's a big place of it for me; in that time, in the transition from living to spirit.

SARA: Do you offer that as a service, Marc?

Dr. Malek: Yeah, we do. It's not something that I've promoted because I generally don't promote euthanasia, but it is something that we offer, not as a paid service, but as something that we contribute to the clients within the practice. The other thing, which is not patient-related that I mentioned before is that Nicki's owner ended up pursuing Reiki through the connection she made to it from all of this and recently became a level 2 Reiki practitioner, and her whole life has changed. She's a completely different person, very much more confident. She's retired. She has a wonderful life going on, and she's even wanted to come in and volunteer. She hasn't yet, but I'm sure she will. That just goes to show that what you least expect might even be the main reason that you're providing treatment at that time, the highest good.

SARA: That was an amazing story. Do you have time for more?

Dr. Malek: Yes, definitely.

Okay. Sassy's a good one too. Sassy was a cat I've seen here, again, I think pretty much all her life. She ended up developing a middle ear tumor that was ... well, the owners weren't going to put her through surgery. She was 14 or 15 at the time. We treated her with a combination of medical protocols and Reiki—steroids, antibiotics, anti-nausea medication, and then Reiki twice a week.

At first, she was really reluctant to come to the practice, as she has been forever, basically. After about three weeks of Reiki therapy, she started eating better, acting better. The owners were amazed at the change in her demeanor and her quality of life. That lasted—it was a number of months, I know for sure, maybe even up to six months that she was doing okay. She also started getting into the carrier—which she hated before. But she started to literally get in the carrier on the days they were going bring her for Reiki.

Then, she'd have Reiki and she would totally love it and fall asleep. And then she'd go home and go take a nap and they'd say she was just energized. She'd run around and be all excited and so on. It really boosted her quality for the time that she had. In fact, on the day that she passed, she had started to decline after a while and they had made the decision to let her go. While she really hadn't tanked, she wasn't living the life that they wanted her to live. She was more quiet and sedentary and what not. They had decided they were going to bring her in, and she just went into the carrier on her own. They just got it out because they were going to take her, and she passed away in the carrier.

Again, while it's not a pleasant ending, it is life. And that's these animals that we treat; they have short lives relative to ours. A large part of that is learning to love them and then loving them and then learning to let them go. Being able to let them go in a way that serves their highest good is just an amazing honor.

SARA: Wow, that's so beautiful. Thank you for sharing that. You're doing such amazing work.

Dr. Malek: Like the many ways that Reiki is being used in your practice, Kathleen, it's so inspiring. If I can take the lead to really let you know that my agenda is to have everyone in my practice Reiki attuned and certified. We're getting there; it's been going through ebbs and flows, losing people and whatnot. By having everybody Reiki attuned and certified, that change that goes on within the individual is something that then, as you guys know, spreads out into the field and throughout the location where you are, as well as into the broader area geographically. However you want to look at it on a material level. It just spreads; it's diffusion.

For me, to have the whole practice be marinating in that energy is what my goal is— because it's like walking into a healing, energetic zone. You're already being treated before you're even receiving the intention of being treated. It also affects human kind and the planet. It sounds grandiose, but as you all know, it starts with one and it works its way out. That's where I am, that's my life right now—sharing it with everybody.

SARA: That is powerful and true. Before we end the interview, Marc, is there any other advice that you might like to share with our SARA members and other readers about Reiki in a veterinarian setting?

Dr. Malek: I think that it's natural as veterinary practitioners to want to help our patients and our clients. I believe Reiki is intelligent energy that lifts beings to their highest potential. We do it in general—on an individual basis or on a treatment basis. But in reality, what I try to do and epitomize in my life is to be Reiki constantly, not only for our patients—for everybody that's involved, everyone who we come in contact with.

Something I would love to share is a meditation that I was inspired to create. It is very simple, and the goal of it is to create a meditative state on an eternal basis, so I call it the healer's eternal meditation.

Breathe in compassionate clarity—don't think "compassionate clarity," just breathe it in. I talk to my staff and say, "As you breathe in, think. You have a puppy that's got a wounded paw. What's that feeling you have right there? You know you can help it— that's the compassion. And you know how to help it, that's the clarity. What's that feeling? Breathe in that feeling."

Think of a feeling that represents compassionate clarity. Breathe in, and then simply breathe out loving gratitude.

What do you feel? What is the loving gratitude? For me, what I focus on and what I feel is when I look at my dog Tsoi (Cho-ee). He's lying there on his little beanbag bed, and he's so cute. I think *I just love this dog. I love this dog. I am so grateful he's in my life.* It's that feeling. You breathe in compassionate clarity, breathe out love and gratitude—the feeling of each of those—with each breath. Start off doing it as a short meditation, five minutes or so, then ultimately this meditation becomes your life. Every breath becomes meditation. And every breath is Reiki.

SARA: You made me cry. That was amazing. Just doing that meditation with you and feeling that. When you really truly feel that compassion, it just is a really open hearted space. That was beautiful. Thank you.

Dr. Malek: *If we could get people to just do this on a daily basis, and it wouldn't take the whole world.* It would only take … just thousands to be doing it on a daily basis. It would change the world. Because that's what we need… we need compassion and love.

It's very simple, and it's a solution. Some might say, "Well, that's not going to solve anything." Well, it does though because it starts with one, and it radiates out. We can go on and talk about all the different studies that have been done, the Maharishi effect[24] and so forth; it's there. There's science to back it up and that's where I live really. That's my personal thing now, melding science and spirituality, and

---

24. https://www.mum.edu/tm-research-overview/maharishi-effect/; https://www.mum.edu/about-mum/consciousness-based-education/tm-research/maharishi-effect/Summary-of-13-Published-Studies

Reiki is that spiritual energy that we know is there—we feel it, it's experiential. And the science aspect proves it out in the real material world.

SARA: Exactly. It's just inspiring to hear someone of your caliber and your profession talking like this and sharing this. You don't hear that often unfortunately, but it's so wonderful and encouraging to hear it from you.

Dr. Malek: I am so blessed and so honored to be able to share it. I know that this approach is something that the world at this time is really searching for, and it's really happening. I'm very optimistic, despite all the craziness that goes on. I am optimistic that this ground swelling of spiritual understanding is growing every day.

SARA: Thankfully it is. Well, thank you so much for being with us, Marc. You've given us all something to think about and something for our hearts to feel. I know that it will be valuable to everyone who reads this book. So blessings.

Dr. Malek: Thanks to you, Kathleen.

If you breathe in compassionate clarity, breathe out love and gratitude. The feeling of each of those, with each breath. And start off doing it as a short meditation, five minutes or so, then ultimately that becomes your life.

Every breath is meditation.

And every breath is Reiki.

DR. MARC MALEK IS THE owner of Foothill Farms Veterinary Hospital in Sacramento, California. He is a Certified Veterinary Acupuncturist, Therapeutic Laser Clinician, and a Level 3 Reiki practitioner and instructor.

Known as Dr. Doolittle by many of his clients, Dr. Malek lives his dream every day helping the animals he loves and the people who love them. He graduated from U.C. Davis with a B.S. in Environmental Toxicology in 1986 and in 1990 from the School of Veterinary Medicine. Immediately after graduating, Dr. M began practicing with a mixed animal practice (large and small animals) in the Marysville/Wheatland, California area. When the owner of the practice sold the large animal component, Dr. M moved to Sacramento and began a new challenge as the managing veterinarian for a fast-paced small animal clinic in 1993. The opportunity to purchase Foothill Farms Veterinary hospital trumped a potential surgical residency in 1994.

Dr. M has become an accomplished surgeon and internist, having worked in solo and group practices for over 26 years. Over the last five years, Dr. Malek has dedicated much of his continuing education to integrative practices. Therapeutic laser treatment has been a staple at FFVH since 2011 due to Dr. Malek's early adoption of this rapid physical medicine healing therapy. He received his Certified Veterinary Acupuncturist certification (large and small animals) in April 2014 from Colorado Veterinary Medicine Association's OneHealth SIM Acupuncture course. He and many of the staff have been learning and practicing Animal Reiki since 2012, and Dr. Malek received his level 3 Animal Reiki instructor certification in June 2014.

You may contact Dr. Marc Malek through her website at www.foothillfarmsvh.com

We, as humans, we are a kind of animal, too, and we are not… how can I say this… I am not more than a cat or dog just because I can build a house—that doesn't put me on a higher level than a cat or dog. When we are doing Reiki or ThetaHealing or another practice, and we are connected, we don't see this difference. We are the same.

Ricardo Garé, DVM

BRAZIL

Dr. Ricardo Garé is internationally well known for his work as a holistic veterinarian. As part of his animal practice in Brazil, he uses Reiki and ThetaHealing as well as a particular source of flower essences for his patients. It's very exciting to have an international perspective for our series of veterinarian interviews and most particularly the experiences of this very seasoned and passionate practitioner of holistic healing for animals and people.

SARA: It's wonderful to be able to share your experiences as a holistic veterinarian located in a country other than the United States with our readers, Ricardo. I'd love it if you could start by telling us a little bit about yourself and your background, and how you came to love Reiki for animals and be a veterinarian who practices Reiki.

Dr. Garé: Thank you, Kathleen. I'm so glad to talk about Reiki, ThetaHealing, and flower essences and animals. I graduated from veterinary college in 2002, and right away I realized that the main principles of veterinarian medicine didn't work for me because in college we were taught to treat the symptoms and not the cause. At that time, they didn't think that the cause of diseases in animals could be emotional and mental—in humans and in animals, it was just a physical cause. I never liked this kind of thinking.

So I finished my veterinary college studies, but I was very lost because I didn't know what to do. I began to practice, but I didn't like the way they taught me, so I looked elsewhere and went to a Reiki seminar in 2003. Once I did this very first level of Reiki, I discovered my place in the veterinary field, in veterinary care. I found myself taking care of the animals with Reiki when until then I had been very lost. I couldn't do the traditional kind of care with animals because I didn't believe in that way.

SARA: So you feel that when you began treating animals with Reiki, it was really the first time that you started to see true healing with animals?

Dr. Garé: Yes, yes. I thought it made sense. When I did the Reiki seminar, I remember thinking, "*Yes, now everything makes sense. Things really happen with energy to the emotional and spiritual and mental processes and they affect the physical.*" So I began to add this to my veterinary knowledge. Then I began to use Reiki on animals and treat animals with Reiki. This was so great for me because I found myself in Reiki.

SARA: That's beautiful. Was there a specific experience with one animal that really just changed your life and made you know that you wanted to focus on Reiki in your practice?

Dr. Garé: Yes, the very first animal that I was going to take care of in a professional way. It was a dog named Babu. It was a stray dog that a family was taking care of. This dog was old and he had a cancerous tumor, a hemangiosarcoma.[25] It's a bad form of cancer, very aggressive, that mostly occurs in dogs. This family chose not to treat with chemotherapy. They chose to only treat with Reiki. I said, "You can treat with chemotherapy plus Reiki. It's okay. We can protect his body from the side effects of chemotherapy with Reiki." But they chose to treat only with Reiki with me.

This was my first Reiki experience as a professional, as a veterinarian, on a dog. I did a Reiki treatment. We usually learn about Reiki in humans with the hand positions, but when we are doing Reiki with animals, they often prefer to walk, to play; sometimes they come near, and we can put our hands on them, and then they will rest far away from us.

This first time I was not yet fully experienced in the way of Reiki because I thought that I needed to put my hands on the dog to give the Reiki, but this dog didn't like that so much—these hand positions. He would walk and then lie near me, but he didn't like my hand position way of doing it. So I needed to stop doing it that way, and I began to figure out how I could offer a better way of giving Reiki to animals.

Because of this very aggressive form of cancer, I was doing Reiki for this dog twice a week. The first thing I saw

---

25. http://www.acvim.org/Portals/0/PDF/Animal%20Owner%20Fact%20Sheets/Oncology/Onco%20Hemangiosarcoma.pdf

was that when I came back for the second time, the second treatment in the same week, this family told me very happily that Babu had returned to being the dog that he was: happy and eating and drinking and running. This was so amazing to me because it was after just one session of Reiki. Then I did the second and the third. I think in two weeks or three, the tumor stopped growing, just with Reiki, and then in maybe three months, it began to shrink. Then after four months of treatment, the tumor had vanished.

This dog was cured of this very aggressive form of cancer with just Reiki. I thought *I'm a veterinarian using Reiki on an animal with cancer, and just Reiki*, and this was so impressive for me.

Wow. Yes, absolutely. So that was where it began. That was a pretty awesome first experience. Yes. My first time with Reiki as a professional, yeah!

SARA: What a beginning! So now, can you tell us about what your practice looks like? In our series of conversations with veterinarians, we have had veterinarians who have had a variety of different types of practices over their careers. I know that you and I have talked before about your practice, which is very special and could even be described as unique. Can you talk a little bit about what holistic modalities you offer, and how you work with your clients?

Dr. Garé: Yes. I work with Reiki, ThetaHealing, Animal Communication and Florais de Saint Germain (Saint Germain Flowers Essences), whose flowers come mainly from Brazil. These protocols are the only ones that use. I don't use allopathy in my work. My main practice is Reiki, Animal

Communication and ThetaHealing, because even when I'm using Reiki, I use the animal communication and some ThetaHealing techniques for discovering limiting beliefs.

So I can talk to animals and find out what their problems are. Sometimes they want things that the family doesn't know about. I talk to the animals about all of this. As a result, often I have some messages for the members of the family that the animal want them to know. This is so good and makes a whole difference in the treatment.

Now, I also treat the family, the humans, because I immediately understood that the animal, this dog or cat, can often absorb the energy and the mental and emotional problems of this family, the caretakers. I think that it's necessary or very important that the human needs be treated, too—by me or by another professional.

So we do this whole thing in a holistic way—I treat the dog, the cat, the human—or another professional treats the human. The cats and dogs improve; they get better and generally healthier. Sometimes, and this has happened, a cat has come to me for the second or third treatment, and they look to the human, and I change the treatment. I say to the caretaker, "Well, you are not okay today, so the treatment will be for you, and we will leave the treatment for the cat for another week." I just do the Reiki treatment on the human, and the cat gets better. So this is very clear for me. I'm doing this in my practice as a holistic veterinarian.

SARA: So do you work on your own? Do you ever train other Reiki people to assist you as a team, or how does that work?

Dr. Garé: Yes, I have a team. I sometimes attempt to work online now because I live in Sao Paulo, Brazil, but my clients often live far from there, sometimes in another country. When these clients choose to work with me online, for instance on Skype, it's with me. When the clients choose to have a residential appointment in the home, it's with the other veterinarian.

SARA: Do they also do Reiki, and do they do other modalities?

Dr. Garé: Yes, they do Reiki, ThetaHealing and one of them offers flower essence therapy.

SARA: Do you have another story about a special animal who's been helped with Reiki that you could share with us?

Dr. Garé: Yes, a horse. I was treating this race horse who was going to be euthanized because he was suffering. The horse had been running and had broken his leg. A friend was asked to treat this horse with acupuncture. Then I came with Reiki, and my friend told me, "This horse is aggressive. He has a lot of fear, so don't be in the same room with him because you could be injured." So, okay, I don't need to get near to do Reiki.

I stood in front of everyone, including the jockey, at a horse hospital in Sao Paulo. As I prepared to begin the treatment, this horse turned and faced me, and was staring at me. I raised my hands to offer Reiki, and this horse came along to me, crossing in front of everyone else there, and laid his head in my hands. This was the first time this horse had even seen me. This was very amazing for me, too. Yet I understood that because I respected the horse, the way this horse knew his fears, and this horse trusted me because of this.

He began to walk again. He didn't have to be euthanized. His leg healed. And it was very incredible. This was my second time using Reiki as a veterinarian.

From then on, I had a lot of cases of treating with Reiki and ThetaHealing and the flower essences. It's a way of life for me. Every week I treat a dog or a cat and learn, with that animal, something about my life. Things that I think are hard in my life, this cat or dog shares something that helps me learn more about it, and the same goes for the family, the clients. It's very beautiful using this holistic way of healing with animals.

SARA: So what do other veterinarians in Brazil, or that you meet with in other parts of the world, think about what you're doing? Are they curious? Are they skeptical? Are they supportive? Do they ask you about what you do?

Dr. Garé: Yes. Some believe, and then some do not believe it, but there are a lot of vets supporting this kind of practice. There are a lot of vets that come to the seminars, Reiki seminars and ThetaHealing seminars, to learn this kind of care. It's very beautiful.

Two weeks ago, I had an interview at a vet clinic called Vets for Cancer. They work only with animals with cancer. They invited me to talk about Reiki and this kind of work for animals with cancer. This was very good because this is not a holistic veterinary clinic. This is an allopathic clinic with chemotherapy, electrochemotherapy.

A lot of shelter animals, when we are doing Reiki, come surround me, this cat or dog, and they want to be loved because love is what cures.

We did this live on Facebook, and it was a huge success. It worked out really well, and they want me to talk again about cases and animals using Reiki and ThetaHealing. It's very good to see Reiki and holistic therapies being used with the mainstream veterinarian way of doing.

SARA: Yes. In English, we call that integrative medicine, where we can put it all together so we don't have to give up one to do the other, but instead use all the tools that we have. It's very powerful.

Dr. Garé: Yes, yes. Sometimes, some veterinarians say to me, "I don't know what Reiki is, but my clients told me that someone did Reiki on this animal, and the animal improved—it got healthier. I don't know what Reiki is, so I want to learn. What is this?" This is very beautiful.

SARA: A lot of people who will be reading our conversation are Reiki practitioners who very much want to create professional relationships with their animal's veterinarian or a veterinarian in their area to help them see the benefits of Reiki and to have it become a part of what they do to support the animals. Do you have any advice for Reiki practitioners who want to help veterinarians or get a foot in the door, in the clinic, so to speak?

Dr. Garé: Yes. There's a lot of scientific research about Reiki now. You can use this scientific research to show them that Reiki works in the typical way.

But I think that it's important to work with, to choose

a vet that has a similar way of thinking about animals. Maybe the vet doesn't believe in Reiki, but he or she is similar to you in the way he experiences animals in general. I think it's better to choose this kind of vet instead of a vet whose way of understanding animals is different from my way of seeing these animals. I see these animals, cats and dogs, as equals, in the sense that they have thoughts and feelings just as we do. If a veterinarian doesn't think in this way, I wouldn't choose this veterinarian to work with my animals, and I wouldn't suggest that as a Reiki practitioner wanting to bring Reiki into the practice, that your readers do either.

I think that this is the first thing: choose professionals that you like, and then talk about Reiki, and you can use scientific research, or you can practice Reiki with some animals in the clinic. It's our way of showing them that Reiki works. But if a veterinarian doesn't believe in the possibility of it working, then it's not going to be easy to make him or her think otherwise, to change that way of thinking. Don't try to push something then. I think that it's better to choose other veterinarians, other professionals, because the other professional that believes or is open to believe, will talk with his veterinarian friends, and will talk about the benefits of Reiki. Then we're changing everything, little by little.

SARA: Thank you. That's beautiful. There's one more thing I wanted to ask you about. I was reading an article that you wrote about the research you did for your master's degree, which involved Reiki—the effects of Reiki on animals—and I believe you won an award for it. It's a very wonderful accomplishment, and the article explained how you had a change of heart about the research methods that you had to use. I thought that this would be really important to hear more about because people are so interested in Reiki research. Could you talk a little bit about what research you did, what it showed, and then how you changed your thoughts about research in general through that process?

Dr. Garé: Sure. I studied the effects of Reiki in animals at Sao Paulo University (known in Brazil as USP) veterinary college in the Master of Science program. I studied the inflammatory results of a chronic disease called granulomatous[26] on animals by studying how the animals' immune system responds from the start of inflammation. Then we did Reiki to see what would happen.

After the study was complete, I changed my understanding of the use of animals in research and realized that it was not necessary, but during the research I had not realized it yet. The Reiki treatments influenced the inflammation response in a way that showed that it can be controlled, that it can be more natural. This chronic inflammation is an extreme way for the body to bring balance to the inflammation response of the immune system. We saw that Reiki can bring this balance in a less inflammatory way. The problem was that to create a scientifically acceptable study, I thought I had to use animals, in this case, rats, for this research. Right from the beginning of the research, I did not like this, but I didn't see another way because I although I didn't like, I still assumed that it was necessary. This was my thought when I did this.

---

26. https://www.mayoclinic.org/diseases-conditions/chronic-granulomatous-disease/symptoms-causes/syc-20355817

SARA: That's the way the scientific community works, so if you want to be accepted, you have to use their formula, I guess.

Dr. Garé: Yes. I thought there was no other way of doing this particular level of scientific study. What changed for me is that in the very final stages of writing my thesis, when I did the research and studied how to talk about the research, I began to discover that there *were* other ways to do research with animals, that you can do clinical trials. In those cases, you don't need to use laboratory animals to do the research. For a time, I felt guilty about the study that I had done, but I eventually let that go.

Then I expanded my view and saw that we don't need laboratory animals to study the effects of Reiki or whatever therapies. We can use the same animals that already need this kind of care. So now, if I choose to do research again, I won't use animals in this way because I don't think that they are needed—I don't think that scientific researchers need to use laboratory animals. We can use animals, cat and dogs, for instance, that already have a problem, and we can study in this way.

Nowadays, I could do the same research, but without laboratory rats; I could study cats or dogs that already have some immune system issues, for example. I will see the same results. I can do things differently today because I don't think that the form of research I used for my master's thesis is needed. We don't need to use laboratory animals to do this.

SARA: I think that's a really important conclusion that you've reached, and coming from a veterinarian who's done research, I think it's very important for our community to hear this. For me, personally, I know that whenever I'm working with animals, I am creating a sense of compassion with Reiki, and so there's a bit of a disconnect when you think about how a scientist has to put those feelings aside to complete a study meant to benefit animals and people. I'm really glad that you are sharing your experience with this particular aspect of science, that you're speaking about it, that you're writing about it, for all of us to consider and to think about as we move forward because we do want Reiki to be accepted. We do want more veterinarians and doctors to offer this to humans and animals of course, but I think we have to find a way forward that is compassionate in order to do this the right way.

Dr. Garé: Yes! Yes—to trust yourself that you want to *do* something different, so do something different. Don't listen to others, even if they told you that this is the only way to do it ... No. There are a lot of ways to do something, and we can do research with love and compassion, and choose not to use animals to do this. I was doing Reiki, and I knew that they were going to be killed. We don't need to do this anymore.

SARA: Thank you, Ricardo, for your willingness to speak so personally about this. It's truly beautiful. Before we finish up, do you have any other advice that you'd like to share with our listeners about promoting Reiki in the veterinary community?

Dr. Garé: Yes. We do need to talk about Reiki with other veterinary professionals of course, yet I think that more than teach and talk about Reiki, it's important to talk about the animal consciousness. This cat or dog or horse or whatever animal species, this is a being, a spiritual being living in a body like us. We, as humans, we are a kind of animal, too, and we are not... how can I say this... I am not more than a cat or dog just because I can build a house—that doesn't put me on a higher level than a cat or dog. When we are doing Reiki or ThetaHealing or another practice, and we are connected, we don't see this difference. We are the same.

When we open to this possibility that this animal is of the same importance as I am, we can open to some messages that we can learn from. One time in my practice, a cat told me that he came from the universe, and it was a cat saying this. It was like reading a book of a master. It could be Buddha or someone like Jesus, I don't know, but it was a cat saying this. It's very important to change the veterinary community in the way they see animals because a lot of veterinary professionals don't see the other species as equal with us. It's like we think that we are better than they are, and we are not better. We are different than this species of animal, but we are animals and everyone has the same importance. This is very important to talk about with veterinarians; and of course also talk about Reiki because it works.

SARA: I love that. What a great teacher that cat was. They all are amazing teachers. I think that consciously creating this understanding in our practice every day is a big piece of what we do at Animal Reiki at Shelter Animal Reiki Association—to remember that animals are our teachers, and that animals are healers in their own right as well. I love the way that you say we're all different, but no one is better. That's beautiful.

I think that more than teach and tell about Reiki, we need to talk about Reiki with other veterinary professionals of course, but it's important to talk about the animal cultures. This cat or dog or horse or whatever animal species, this is a being, a spiritual being living in a body like us.

Dr. Garé: When I am doing Reiki at shelters, a lot of shelter animals come and surround me, this cat or that dog, and they want to be loved because love is what heals. It's the same, of course, that humans want to be loved. It's simple. We are not different in this way, and when, for me, we are doing Reiki, this kind of practice, it's love. Some can call it God or creator, but for me, it's called and is love. That's so beautiful. For me, that's the reason why this works, because it's love. It's the same purpose, and humans and cats and dogs need love to live better.

SARA: Beautiful. Thank you so much, Ricardo. Thank you so much for being a part of this special series that we're doing and for educating us about the possibilities of Reiki. Your practice and your work are very inspiring to all of us, so thank you for what you do for the animals through your veterinary practice. It's absolutely beautiful and wonderful. Congratulations for your work.

Dr. Garé: Thank you, Kathleen. I'm very, very glad and very happy to talk about this with you and your readers because your *Animal Reiki* book was very important to me in my practice as a professional with animals doing Reiki.

DR. RICARDO GARÉ graduated Veterinary in 2002 and has had his own Holistic Veterinarian practice since 2003. He received his Master in Reiki degree in 2008, became a ThetaHealing® Instructor in 2017, and a Floral Therapist since 2016. He continues to teach and attend ThetaHealing classes, Animal Communication classes and teaches Reiki seminars for humans as well as Animal Reiki seminars. Dr. Garé also teaches classes about the Florals of Saint Germain.

You may contact Dr. Garé through his website at www.holisticvet-ricardogare.com.

The Tree of Life for Animals (TOLFA)

RAJASTHAN, INDIA

The last section of this book contains commentary written and compiled by Alison McKinnon, the International Director of SARA and one of its teachers, about some of her experiences at The Tree of Life for Animals (TOLFA), a veterinary hospital and rescue center located in Rajasthan, India, where she has given Animal Reiki to some of their patients. The account focuses on a particular surgery and includes the observations of British registered veterinary nurse Rachel Wright, the founder of TOLFA and a 2018 recipient of the Royal College of Veterinary Surgeons' International Award; of Jemma Sadler, assistant manager at TOLFA; and of the attending surgeon, Dr. Aftab Ahmed Khan.

THE TREE OF LIFE FOR ANIMALS (TOLFA) IN Rajasthan, India is a hospital and rescue center founded by British veterinary nurse Rachel Wright in 2018. Rachel advocates the use of complementary therapies at the center, and in 2013 launched a Reiki program following the guidelines of SARA, The Shelter

Animal Reiki Association, whose co-founder Kathleen Prasad promotes the "Let Animals Lead" method. TOLFA hosts training classes and mentors would-be Animal Reiki teachers, as well as offers Reiki to residents and animals there to undergo treatment. TOLFA provides the ideal location for teaching classes as a whole range of cases may come through the gates on an average day—mainly street animals including dogs and cattle, but other common patients include donkeys, pigs, goats, and increasingly, cats. Many, as well as being injured or sick, are understandably stressed at being confined during their stay at the hospital.

It was during one such visit, while mentoring another Reiki practitioner, that I was called away to join the team in the operating room for a young dog that had just been brought in. He had been hit by a train. As I entered the room, the dog was being stabilized by the team, who were bustling around him, and it was clear that he was in shock—his body was a bloody mess, his shoulder was shattered— and it was touch and go as to whether he would make it. The only option to save this dog was to amputate his leg.

To bring Reiki into the medical environment has many uses. Reiki can help calm and lift some of the fear from animals as they are going through the dying process—a spiritual hand to hold as they transition. Conversely, Reiki can provide the spark of energy and support for those who really want to fight to live. The practitioner's role is to offer this connection without judgement or influence for the animal to use as it chooses to, which may be not at all in some cases—it is always up to them. Sometimes the practitioner will receive intuition as to how the animals are feeling as they connect to the energy, and in this particular case the feeling was that this dog very much wanted to survive.

As an experienced practitioner with several visits to India under my belt, one of the key skills I have developed is to stay grounded and calm (using Reiki techniques to achieve that) in these "extreme" situations—you will be of no use to the animal and get in the way of staff if you get upset. Reiki does not require physical touch, so if you feel overwhelmed by what you are seeing in front of you, Reiki can be offered from an adjacent room or outside the building where the animal is being treated, allowing you to more easily focus on the situation inside.

Veterinary surgeon Dr. Khan was happy for me to stay in the room for the operation, which I appreciated as I know he had no idea of what Reiki was or what I was doing there. The operation to remove the damaged leg and carefully stitch together layers of damaged tissue took about two hours, and I was able to channel Reiki during the entire time. My awareness of the energy being used changed from time to time—for example as sedation was being monitored (possibly when the effect of the drugs was wearing off, as gas anesthesia is not available), he responded to the energy being offered. This also occurred as the leg was removed. I was aware of energy being directed to the healthy tissue at a cellular level. This is not an unusual occurrence. When offering Reiki, the practitioner may intuitively feel what is happening, but it is by no means necessary to direct or send energy; in fact, it is important to focus on just offering Reiki, pure and simple, with no attachment to the outcome—a sometimes difficult skill to learn.

Not expecting any feedback from Dr. Khan, I was pleased to hear that he was interested in the fact that the dog's temperature had stayed constant during the surgery and in recovery and that when coming round, he seemed alert but also unusually quiet and calm considering the horrific injuries he had sustained and how much blood he had lost. Reiki is being used more and more in the human medical setting with research showing that it can help patients manage anxiety and post-op pain, and this would appear to be the case with animals too.

Rachel later reported to me that he did indeed recover very

quickly. However, during his convalescence he had a reaction to medication, and he was again very receptive to Reiki given by assistant manager Jemma Sadler. This is a great example of why I think it is a wonderful gift for the patients to have members of a vet staff be open to learning Reiki for themselves.

This dog is now a permanent resident at TOLFA and has been named Three Wheeler no. 2, in memory of one of Rachel's beloved shelter dogs, the original Three Wheeler.

Jemma Sadler, Assistant Project Coordinator at TOLFA, described her role in the story of Three Wheeler no. 2 and Reiki.

My experience with Three Wheeler no. 2 took place while he was recovering from his operation when he suddenly began to have an allergic reaction to an antibiotic he had been given. The reaction resembled anaphylactic shock: his airways began to swell, causing them to start to close off, which of course meant that it became very difficult for him to breathe in a very short space of time. I ended up sitting on the floor with him with his head in my lap, offering him Reiki whilst he was being given medical treatment to ease the breathing problems. At one point, his breathing became so labored that we actually thought we were going to lose him, and I clearly remember feeling extra Reiki energy being sent at that time to help him in whichever way he needed.

Happily for Three Wheeler, he did pull through, and I do believe that the Reiki he was offered at that time supported him and gave him the strength to make it through the period when the allopathic medicine was beginning to work.

Sometime after the surgery, I asked Dr. Khan whether he had on thoughts about Three Wheeler's surgery, and although it had been one of many that this doctor performs at the center, he did remember it and had these comments to make.

Dr. Khan said that he did remember the operation because it involved such a fresh, traumatic wound. The one thing he remembers being most surprised by was how Three Wheeler's vital signs such as his heart rate, blood pressure, and breathing seemed to be very stable considering the immense trauma of his injury, the pain he must have been in before we got to him, and the shock from the accident and from the amount of blood he had already lost. He also found Alison's presence in the operation theatre to be very calming and that the feeling continued throughout the operation. He referenced this in particular because when conducting emergency surgery such as this was, often experiencing this kind of calmness is not the case simply due to the time pressures involved in trying to save an animal in such dire condition.

Animal Reiki Practitioner Code of Ethics

DEVELOPED BY KATHLEEN PRASAD, FOUNDER OF ANIMAL REIKI SOURCE

GUIDING PRINCIPLES:

- I believe the animals are equal partners in the healing process.

- I honor the animals as being not only my clients, but also my teachers in the journey of healing.

- I understand that all animals have physical, mental, emotional and spiritual aspects, to which Reiki can bring profound healing responses.

- I believe that bringing Reiki to the human/animal relationship is transformational to the human view of the animal kingdom.

- I dedicate myself to the virtues of humility, integrity, compassion and gratitude in my Reiki practice.

IN WORKING ON MYSELF, I FOLLOW THESE PRACTICES:

- I incorporate the Five Reiki Precepts into my daily life and Reiki practice.

- I commit myself to a daily practice of self-healing and spiritual development so that I can be a clear and strong channel for healing energy.

- I nurture a belief in the sacred nature of all beings, and in the value and depth of animal kind as our partners on this planet.

- I listen to the wisdom of my heart, remembering that we are all One.

IN WORKING WITH THE ANIMALS, I FOLLOW THESE GUIDELINES:

- I work in partnership with the animal.

- I always ask permission of the animal before beginning, and respect his or her decision to accept or refuse any treatment. I listen intuitively and observe the animal's body language in determining the response.

- I allow each animal to choose how to receive his or her treatment; thus each treatment could be a combination of hands-on, short distance and/or distant healing, depending on the animal's preference.

- I let go of my expectations about how the treatment should progress and/or how the animal should behave during the treatment, and simply trust Reiki.

- I accept the results of the treatment without judgment and with gratitude toward Reiki and the animal's openness and participation in the process.

IN WORKING WITH THE HUMAN COMPANIONS OF THE ANIMALS, I WILL:

- Share information before the treatment about my healing philosophy, the Reiki healing system and what to expect in a typical treatment, as well as possible outcomes, including the possibility of healing reactions.

- Provide a clear policy ahead of time regarding fees, length of treatment and cancellation policy, as well as "postponement" policy, should the animal not want the treatment that day.

- Never diagnose. I will always refer clients to a licensed veterinarian when appropriate.

- Honor the privacy of the animals and their human companions.

- Share intuition received during Reiki treatments, with compassion and humility, for the purpose of supporting their understanding of the healing process.

- Respect the human companion's right to choose the animal's healing journey, selecting the methods, both holistic and/or conventional that he or she deems most appropriate, with the support and advice of a trusted veterinarian.

IN WORKING IN THE COMMUNITY, I HOLD THE FOLLOWING GOALS:

- I model the values of partnership, compassion, humility, gentleness and gratitude in my life and with the animals, teaching by example.

- I work to create professional alliances and cooperative relationships with other Reiki practitioners/teachers, animal health-care providers and animal welfare organizations in my community.

- I strive to educate my community in its understanding of the benefits of Reiki for animals.

- I continually educate myself to maintain and enhance my professional competence so that I uphold the integrity of the profession.

- I consider myself an ally to the veterinary and animal health community. I work to support their efforts in achieving animal wellness and balance. I honor other disciplines and their practitioners.

The Shelter Animal Reiki Association

SARA

THE SHELTER ANIMAL REIKI ASSOCIATION (SARA) is a non-profit organization that teaches and promotes the Let Animals Lead™ method which uses meditation practices. Our goal is to create a peaceful, healing environment within shelters and other animal care settings. We work closely with staff and volunteers of shelter/rescues, veterinarians, and service organizations to help create a positive healing space for all.

We are a group of Reiki practitioner and teacher volunteers committed to supporting rescued animals and their caregivers with the healing benefits of Reiki meditation. Reiki can help animals become more adoptable, and help their caretakers stay strong and calm in even the most difficult situations. Reiki meditation can support all aspects of healing.

For more information, visit us at
www.shelteranimalreikiassociation.org.

Made in the USA
Middletown, DE
03 July 2019